Leopards, Oracles, and Long Horns

Three West African Epic Cycles:
***

Kingdon of the Leopard
Oracles Don't Lie
Land of the Long Horn

By

chichi layor

Panther  Creek Press
Spring, Texas

Copyright © 2001 by chichi layor okoye
All rights reserved including the right to reproduction in whole or in part in any form

Published by Panther Creek Press
116 Tree Crest Circle
P.O. Box 130233
Panther Creek Station
Spring, Texas 77393

Cover design by Pamela Copus,
Sonic Media; Plano, Texas

Manufactured in the United States of America
Printed and bound by Data Duplicators, Inc.,
Houston, Texas

1 2 3 4 5 6 7 8 9 10

Library of Congress Cataloguing in Publication Data

layor, chichi
    Leopards, Oracles and Long Horns

1. Title   2. Poetry   3. Epic   4. West Africa   5. Edo   6. Yoruba   7. Hausa

ISBN 0-9678343-3-3

To the memory of my father,
Mokwugo Okoye

Leopards, Oracles and Long Horns could not have been researched and written without the assistance of a number of people, some of whose names I have forgotten in the ten or so years since the book was conceived.

To my publisher, editor, agent, mentor and adviser, Dr. Guida Jackson, who conceived this project and saw it through to fruition, I am immensely grateful for her unflagging encouragement and unwavering optimism during those incredibly long years of waiting for the book to be born. Special thanks are due to Joyce Harlow who worked tirelessly behind the scenes, and to Pamela Copus, who designed the book cover. For his gracious help and encouragement despite a busy schedule, I am sincerely grateful to Professor Ernest Emenyonu in North Carolina (USA).

Many thanks to: Justice Joan Aiwerioghene in Benin City (Nigeria) for taking great interest in my work and helping me to gather materials; Dr. E. Imasuen in Benin City and Dr. Rina Okonkwo in Enugu (Nigeria) for kindly lending me books which aided my research.

No words can adequately express my profound gratitude for the unstinting support on many levels that I received from my beloved parents, Mokwugo and Ifeoma Okoye, in Enugu during the gestation period of this book; unfortunately, my father didn't live to see its birth. To my writer-parents I owe my incurable reading habit, my great love of words and writing as well as my astigmatism.

Finally, I am deeply indebted to my dear husband Andrew Archbold for his helpful and frank suggestions, his untiring patience and unconditional love during the final stages of the production of this book.

chichi layor
chichi_99@lycos.com

TABLE OF CONTENTS
***

THE KINGDOM OF THE LEOPARD

Tales of Old Benin

INTRODUCTION

The people of Benin are called Binis, and the ancient Benin Empire extended beyond Nigeria to Dahomey (now Republic of Benin). Today the Binis are only found in Mid-west Nigeria

The Binis generally believed in many gods: Osanobua, the supreme god; Ogiuwu, god of death; Ekoko, and others.

The Oba of Benin is the head of the Benin Kingdom, and he is highly revered. The Binis operate a monarchy which does not allow women to rule. The King lives in Benin City which is the capital of the Benin Empire. He only comes out on special occasions, and his wives are also congined to the palace, where they are not allowed to receive men expect for relatives.

The heir apparent is invested with the title of Edaiken of Uselu, and he must live in Uselu until he is crowned Oba.

The Iyase (Prime Minister) of Benin was the Commander-in-Chief during wars and the Ezomo was second in command, the generalissimo of the state army and the overlord of Uzebu, a quarter in the city. He is of the same rank as the Edaiken (the Crown Prince).

The Iyoba or Queen Mother is the only female who can contribute to state affairs.

The Oliha is the chief whose duty is to crown the king.

Every title in Benin is conferred by the Oba. Usually a titled man is known by his title, and titled chiefs are generally highly respected.

Coral beads feature prominently in the King's costume--they are made into necklaces, ankets, crowns and royal robes. The Oba also bestows coral beads on his chiefs, who must wear them around their necks while in the Oba's presence.

*EDITOR'S NOTES

The beginnings, some six or seven centuries ago, of the Edo (Iyekovin) kingdom of Benin--not related to the present-day Republic of Benin--are lost in legend. Although West African oral tradition often adheres closely to historical fact, on the subject of Benin's earliest rulers, discrepancies exist between lists collected in the latter part of the 19th century, those of the official historian of Benin some thirty-five years ago, and that collected more recently from Isekhurhe, the priest of the royal ancestors. It seems certain, however, that the earliest kingship at Benin predated Sundiata (king of Mandinkan Kangaba) by a century and Mansa Musa (king of Mali) by two centuries.

A study by linguists of the Edo of Benin has led to the conclusion that the forest inhabitants of 14th century Benin (when by every account Benin had been flourishing for a century, probably two) were descended from ancestors who had lived in the area since the remote Stone Age. The kingdom, eventually encompassing an area between the Niger Delta and Lagos, is thought to have drawn its political institutions from Ife and other neighboring Yoruba states.

Some tradition holds that Benin was founded by Obagodo, a son of Oduduwa, the semi-mythical Yoruba patriarch, founder of Ife, the first Yoruba kingdom and the Yoruba holy city. Obagodo became ruler of Benin as Ogiso, or king. Intrigues by his senior wife caused Ogiso to banish his only son Kalderhan, who later declined to return to rule until the chiefs sent to Oduduwa, requesting that he send another prince. Oduduwa sent another son, Oranmiyan (or Oranyan), who married a local princess and sired a son, Eweka. When Eweka came of age, Oranmiyan returned to Ife, leaving his son as the first oba of Benin. It is the date of Oranmiyan's entry into Benin's history that the first serious descrepancy appears. Eghareuba's *Short History* (see king list) gives the date as 1300, while the priest Esekhurhe maintains the date as 1170. The dates in the following text will be Esekhurhe's, although Eghareub's list is given.

Under Eweka and his two successors, the oligarchical power of the chiefs increased. When Ewedo came to power (ca. 1255), he contended with the rebellious chiefs under the leadership of Ofiamwe by moving the capital, and by stripping away some of the nobles' power. It is Ewedo who is credited with devising the tripartite hierarchy of chiefs designed to limit their power. The highest ranking were the hereditary noblemen, called the uzama, who were the princes with their own fiefs, who chose the oba. Next were the town chiefs, consisting of religious and military leaders, who were more popular than the uzama simply because they were not leaders by heredity. The third-ranked chiefs were palace chiefs chosen by the reigning oba.

Ewedo is also credited with renaming the kingdon Ubini, from which Benin is derived.

Under his son Oguola (or Ogwola), bronze workers were imported from Ife to fashion weapons for use in an ongoing war against Udo, west of the River Ovia. It was Oguola who initiated the famous Benin sculptures which tradition says he ordered designed to record historical events.

Under Udagbedo (or Dagbedo), the kingdom was expanded over much of lower present-day Nigeria and as far as Accra, in Ghana. Sickness, weakness, or lameness disqualified a ruler, so when Udagbedo became infirm, he hid the fact from his subjects, until his prime minister discovered the deception and he was forced to resign.

After a succession of weak leaders, Ewuare the Great (r. ca. 1440-1480), of layor's poem "ikpoba river", having murdered his brother Uwaifiokun who had usurped the throne, became an oba of great power, expanding the kingdom, becoming the overlord of seven lesser kings, according to accounts by Portuguese who came to arrange trade agreements: Benin's pepper for guns. Benin also became one of the largest suppliers of Ibo slaves. Ewuare was said to employ magic to extend Benin's influence beyond the Edo-speaking regions. In addition to being a great warrior-magician, Ewuare was a lover of beauty. He introduced the wind instrument Eziken and wood and ivory carving, bringing the famed carver Egboghomiaghen to Benin.

Following Ewuare's death, his successor Ezoti lasted only fourteen days before he died. According to K. Madhu Panniker, Ezoti's brother Okpame had Ezoti's eldest son and chief wife murdered and usurped the throne. Although an enraged populace soon drove him out, Ezoti (Olua, mentioned in layor's second poem) feared to accept the throne, and thus it was offered to the eldest daughter; layor's poem "why women don't rule in benin" gives a description of the ensuing events. Eventually Olua ruled briefly, and after an Iwu threat, the commoners recalled Okpame to the throne. He took the name Ozolua the Conqueror and defeated both the Iwe and his own nobles, but during the battle a poison arrow ended his life.

Two sons, by different wives, vied to replace him. Osawe, younger by a few hours, acceded under the name Esigie (r. ca. 1504-1550), subject of layor's "imaguero' and "master thief." His mother, Idia, who fought in the Igala war and became Iye Oba (Queen Mother), is the subject of "a battle and a dance."

Esigie was a colorful oba who, during a war against Idah (1515-1518), sent an ambassador to Purtugal. The ambassador returned with missionaries. The oba ordered his son and two great noblemen to become Christian and built a church in Benin. They learned to read, and the oba himself became conversant in Portuguese. In 1540, he sent the Portuguese king a brass crucifix, but Benin and its subsequent rulers did not embrace Christianity, and soon its obas reverted to magical rituals and human sacrifices as protection.

Some ten obas ruled in the next two centuries. Among them, Ozolua (r. fl. 1481) appears in layor's "ise and oba ozolua"; Ehengbudy (r. fl. 1578) in layor's "ekpenede"; Akengbedo (r. fl. 1675) in "adesua"; and Ewuakpe (r. ca. 1685 or 1700) in her third poem. The royal line reigned undisturbed in Benin City until 1897, when the British Consul in the Niger Coast Protectorate was killed by Benin warriors of Oba Overami Ovonramwen, formerly Idugbowa, subject of layor's first poem), who claimed the Consul had intruded on a sacred ceremony. Under Queen Victoria's orders, Overami was exiled, the city ransacked of some 2500 bronzes and burned, and the kingdom virtually dismantled.

Overami died in Calibar in 1914, and his son petitioned the British king for permission to assume the throne. He took the name Eweka II with greatly reduced powers. Descendants continue to occupy the throne in Benin City, having only an advisory role.

Other of layor's always lively poems cannot be dated, as they relate adventures of persons, often women, not mentioned in our available historical texts. These poems do, however, provide additional windows into the colorful life of the Kingdom of the Leopard.

The following list is from Egareuba, J. U., *A Short History of Benin.* Lagos, Nigeria (1936) pp. 85-86

Egharevba's King List

1300	Oranmiyan
	Eweka I
1340	Uwakhuahen
	Ehenmihen
1370	Ewedo
1400	Oguola
	Edoni
	Udagbedo
1430	Ohen
1450	Egbeka
	Orobiru
	Uwaifiokun
	Ewuare
1475	Ezoti [Edeleyo, female, briefly]
	Olua
1480	Ozolua
1520	Esigie
	Orhogbua
1570	Ehengbuda
1610	Ohuan
1630	Ahenzae
1650	Akenzae
1670	Akengboi
	Akenkpaye
	Akengbedo
	Ore-Oghene
1685	Ewuakpe
1715	Ozuere
	Akenzua I
1740	Eresoyen
1760	Akengbuda
1803	Obanosa
	Ogbebo
1815	Osemwede
1852	Adolo
1888	Ovonramwen
	Eweka II
	Azenzua II

10

KINGDOM OF THE LEOPARD

Tales from Old Benin

oba overami

in the sight of his subjects
the king was a god
the home-leopard of the benin race
tall and light-skinned
with a voice like thunder
the oba was defiant daring and proud

three white men came calling at his palace one day
with gifts from the exquisite british queen
and a trade treaty to be signed
the oba refused gifts and treaty both
seeing in the gifts a trojan horse

oba overami consulted an oracle
who saw heavy shadows hanging over his reign
and fire and blood
engulfing the empire
so the oba swore he'd tighten sevurity

years later more white men came
at a most inconvenient time
the period of the iguen festival
when obas did not receive visitors
especially from a foreign land
so decreed the benin tradition

the oba sent his chief warlord
to check the march of the white men
until the festival was over
and he could receive them albeit reluctantly

but news soon came that the visitors were dead

11

the oba's warlord in defense of the killing
reported that the visitors defied his orders
and advanced beyond a given point

on advice of his prime minister
the oba prepared for war
as the british were bound to avenge their dead

angry troops bombarded benin
resolving to rout the oba
with superior military might
the oba's men fought valiantly
but were mowed down like grass
so that survivors escaped into the bushes
leaving behind gruesome scenes
of decapitated and decomposing bodies
fire and blood the oracle said
fire and blood in benin city

finally the home-leopard went into hiding
battered and beaten
but the british troops ferreted him out

during the court trial
he merely mopped his brow
calm and composed in the face of fierce threats
from the consul-general

the oba denied ordering the visitors' deaths
his warlord had acted of his own will
but the consul-general apparently unimpressed
banished the oba to calabar
where he'd be taught anew to rule

of his huge harem he was allowed only three
the rest had to remain in benin
thus broken and bowed the oba died
a commoner's death in calabar

emotan

in the powerful kingdom of benin
during the reign of oba ohen
lived a young girl called elere
although a beauty she was most unhappy
for her father would have her marry the oliha
but she craved the oba instead
so she saw her lover on the sly

one day when the oba visited her
she wept silently and sadly
for soon she must marry the oliha against her will
and never would she meet the king again

but oba ohen had a brilliant idea
and he wanted elere
how he wanted her
so he wiped her tears away
and doused her doubts with this foolproof plan

while ekoko dancers entertained that night
the lovers would borrow two sets of clothes and masks
and dance disguised to the oba's palace
with the real ekoko dancers in tow
who'd follow the lovers into the palace
take back their clothes and masks
and resume their riotous dancing
so no one would know anything was amiss

everything went according to plan
and oba ohen married elere
thus outwitting the oliha

after their son was born
elere's love for the oba waxed cold
and like the setting sun she slipped away
to her village
and the oba never saw her again

she had a cousin in another village
her name was uwaraye
and she was very beautiful

uwaraye was so beautiful
you could look at her all day long and marvel
at her dark deep eyes
at her smooth olive-like skin
and her voice that tinkled and trilled

she could spin thread and make melon butter
for her mother had taught her these skills
hoping she'd make some man a wonderful wife
uwaraye was their only living child
they longed to have grandsons and a son-in-law

scores of suitors came to uwaraye's door
drooling and dreaming for her beauty was dazzling
but she did not give them a glance
at the sight of a suitor she ran away
for she loved her parents so particularly
she hated having to part from them

she could spin thread finer than cobwebs
singing as she spun in a sonorous voice
she sold yarn in the village market
so profitably her parents were pleased
but she was slow and hated housework
a girl is entitled to at least one flaw

she continued to spurn her suitors' offers
so her father chose the azama
a man of royal blood
but the ravishing girl remained unmoved

finally her father enforced his decision
and the azama took uwaraye away
to the kingdom of benin
as his second wife

his first wife arabe was secretly resentful
of the beautiful new wife he'd acquired
and though arabe was unfriendly and forbidding
the azama himself was quite kind

but uwaraye was unhappy there
for she had no children while arabe had plenty
and taunted her saying she was good-for-nothing
and because she served her meals very late
the azama renamed her emotan
meaning lazy and slow

II

now oba ohen had ruled for twenty years
he was handsome but not very healthy
his right leg became lame
such a crying shame
for the oba of benin was held in high esteem
like a god he was faultless and free from human failings

so he kept his lameness from the people
but his closest servants were in the know
for they carried the oba where he wanted to go
the oba's second-in-command was the iyase

and he was baffled by the king's behavior
for the oba declined to see visitors
and at special ceremonies that required his presence
he'd be first to arrive and last to leave
so his servants could carry him in secret

some strange stories began to spread
some said the oba was sick
some said he was bewitched
finally the country was in disarray

the iyase decided to so something

(he was prime minister after all)
to root for the reason the oba always arrived early at ceremonies

the iyase hid behind a door
waiting for the ceremony to begin
while servants carried the oba into the hall
the iyase watched through a hole in the door
but he was spotted by the royal guards
and brought before oba ohen

the oba was rabid ranting and raving
and ordered the express execution of the iyase
the other chiefs were terror-stricken
and vowed to get rid of oba ohen

for years they plotted and planned the oba's death

one day a pit was dug beneath his throne
and covered with brittle wood and a white cloth
the following day being a festival day
the chiefs in their ceremonial robes
stood around the oba's throne
each man clutching a lump of white chalk

ensconced in his ancient throne
the oba made a sudden move
and crashed clumsily into the pit
where the chiefs and the people stoned him to death
thus ridding theselves of their erratic king

fierce fighting followed the oba's death
his killers versus his former allies

the oba had four sons from different women
and each was to rule benin in turn
but three sons were weak and the one who was strong
was ogun the son of elere the oba's runaway wife

the chiefs wanted a king they could manipulate
so they got ogun's second brother to send him away

16

and the brother became oba
prince ogun was in exile when the oba died
and though he was the next-in-line
he could not be found
so his youngest brother became the new oba

in the meantime the azama died
thus rendering emotan homeless
for custom decreed that only his children could inherit his property
so arabe and her children took over the house

but emotan did not twiddle her thumbs
she took up trading once more
selling melon butter in oba market
as the market grew
emotan's fame spread
for she was warm-hearted
and good with children
often baby-sitting for busy mothers

although she had none of her own
children loved her and gathered round her
she had come to be known as
the queen of oba market

the aging emotan was troubled
by the goings-on in the land
during the reign of prince ogun's kid brother
so she prayed fervently for ogun's return

one evening when the market was closed
an unkempt man stopped at emotan's shop
and begged her for a little food
she was tired and hungry herself
but shared her meagre rations with the raggedy man
who in gratitude revealed his true self
as prince ogun the long-lost heir

he'd returned to take his rightful place
as the oba of benin
emotan warned him of the spies his brother sent everywhere

17

and ogun seeking to know on whose side the chiefs were on
went to see a certain chief ogiefa

the chief while warning him to beware of the oba's spies
treacherously fetched the oba's men
but the chief's head slave helped ogun get away
and he took refuge in emotan's hut

the oba was informed of ogun's return
and his spies strained every nerve in their search
killing anyone suspected of aiding ogun

emotan went round rallying supporters of ogun
they got their weapons ready
and awaited his signal to attack
while they communicated through emotan with him

emotan found out that a ceremony would be held the following week
when the oba's procession would pass by her market
so ogun planned to dispatch the oba as he went by
surrounded by drummers and dancers

on that day ogun watched from emotan's hut
as the procession drew nearer and nearer
singing praise songs to the unsuspecting oba
dispatch dancers running to and fro
waved their swords in the air
some secretly hating the oba intensely

nearer and nearer the oba came
gloriously decked out in customary gear
arms encased in ivory bands
neck ringed with coral beads
raffia hanging thickly from waist

beaded crown upon his head
as two chiefs supported him on each side
he trudged along
blissfully unaware that one of the dancers was ogun

a momentary rebuke
gave the oba no time to reply
and then ogun sank a spear
into his brother's chest
fast felling him
so that the chiefs fled
and ogun won his people's loyalty at last
he was crowned oba of benin
ewuare the great

poor emotan died before ogun was crowned

she didn't live to see her dream come true
oba ewuare deified her
for her kindness and great courage
he planted a tree in her memory
and people came to her grave to pray
offering all kinds of gifts to her
thus did they honor emotan

today a life-sized statue marks the sacred grave
replacing the tree that was planted for her
cast in bronze the statue stands tall
near the oba market in benin city.

iden and oba ewuakpe

the queen mother died
and 800 souls were buried with her
at the king's command

the benin people rose in rebellion
and removed the oba
stripping him of slaves
wives
sword bearers
bodyguards
everything

his senior wife iden stood firm
as the palace was sacked by the populace
and the oba's former chiefs were floored
by this woman with a man's courage
so they said

the oba lamented the loss of this throne
the power and privileges that he'd had
slowly his life was ebbing away
when iden suggested he consult an oracle
so he did

the oracle said
he could revocer his crown
by sacrificing someone to the gods
but who would be that sacrifice?

no slaves remained in the palace now
no one but his wife iden
so whom would the oba sacrifice?

the question kept him awake at night
only a step away from his lost glory
but who oh who would be that step?

eureka
the answer came
iden offered to be the sacrifice

the oba protested
and his wife insisted
saying it was the only way to go
as he couldn't remain a commoner

his was loath to sacrifice his wife
for power
but she in selfless love
urged him to accept her sacrifice
with one condition only
that her death be commemorated yearly

finally his reluctance wore thin
and she was buried alive
instantly he regained his throne
and his subjects paid homage to him
once again

today iden is remembered
for her loyalty

a battle and a dance

during oba esigie's reign
the king of idah planned to attack benin
but news reached the oba
through his sedulous spies

he told his mother idia
he would invade idah
but she told him to stay home
and let her fight instead

the oba maintained he should fight
not she
but idia was raring to go
as her slave held her
begging her to stay
she drew her dagger
and swiftly slew him

laden with daggers and guns and all
idia and her troops marched on idah
where they soon subdued the king

idia fought on
ignoring the idahs' desperate pleas
until they staged a special dance
to placate her
the ekassa dance

she had never seen
a dance so colorful
she simply gaped in glee
and invited the dancers to benin

they went with her
and she showed them to her son
saying that her one desire
was that the dance be performed
at her burial ceremony

she got her wish
and every year she gets her dance

who'd have believed
a dance could end a bloody war?

imaguero

as a token of friendship
oba esigie gave his daughter in marriage
to his warlord the oliha

all went well until the warlord
took a new wife
imaguero
thus bringing the number of his wives to five

suddenly
the oba warned his warlord against women
saying they were not to be trusted
for they were sneaky and sly
even toward their lords and masters

when the oliha declared imaguero
the most faithful wife in all of benin
the oba crowed in mocking laughter
that echoed around the palace walls
and back

before the chiefs and elders the oba told
of how he'd sent a servant with mouth-watering gifts
to imaguero who fell for the bait
and the gift-bearer
thus betraying her husband's trust

chafing the warlord challenged the king
to a duel
in a bid to settle the thorny matter
once and for all
but the duel was a draw

the oba's taunts rankled
and the oliha was now ravaged by doubt
yet he loved imaguero
was he wild about her
it made the other wives murderous
not least of all the king's daughter

bristling the warlord sent for all his wives
and in accordance with custom
he drew a confession
from his princess-wife
who admitted that jealousy pushed her to plot with her father
against imaguero

impervious to her pleading
the oliha killed her

it was time for truth-telling
so imaguero took her turn
swearing by the shrine of her father-in-law
she told the oliha a tearful tale

one evening when the warlord was out
oba esigie sent a servant to me bearing gifts and a message:
the king desired me
i told the scared servant it was unthinkable
that i break my marriage vows
even if he was the oba

chichi layor

he wasn't my husband
he servant soon returned with a threat
my parents would be killed
if i didn't yeild to the oba's demands
befuddled and afraid
i visited my parents with your permission
and they sadly agreed i give in
to save their lives and yours

so i did
my poor husband
it seems that i must die

the oliha was devastated
and a trifle disbelieving
but imaguero insisted
she had to die
and in vain did her husband curse the oba
in vain did he speak to her of his love
in vain did he assure her of complete pardon
imaguero declared she couldn't live with the guilt

drinking poison
she died in the warlord's arms

adesua

the ezomo had a beautiful daughter
called adesua
betrothed to oba akengbuda

one day a prince was crowned in benin
as the obi of oboro-uku
in accordance with custom he called on the ezomo
who presented him with kolanuts
through his lovely daughter
instantly the obi wooed her
but her jeering laughter jabbed into his chest
as she called him a bush ruler

the obi bridled with anger
and when he got home
he put a spell on adesua
so that she came to oboro-uku market
to demand a debt that was owed her

when the obi sent for her
she spurned his advances
again
in a busy market
this time

now he went stark raving mad
and had her killed
for hell hath no fury like a man scorned

news of adesua's death reached her father
and he went to see the oba
who decided to avenge her death
at once

oba akengbuda sent his troops to war
against oboro-uku town
after fierce fighting
the obi was killed
and his head sent to the oba
as a gift

why women don't rule in benin

when oba ewuare died
his eldest son ezoti was killed on coronation day
and heir apparent
ezoti's eldest son
was killed by oba ewuare's third son
ozolua

the murderer was banished from the empire

leaving oba ewuare's second son
but he was spineless and scared of ozolua
and didn't care to be crowned king

so the people decided to crown ewuare's eldest daughter
edeleyo
who was beautiful and rich
just perfect for the post
so she was given the title of edaiken
as a pre-coronation ritual

coronation day came
and fully-dressed in royal regalia
complete with escorts
she began her trek to uselu village

en route she was overtaken by
a sudden illness
quick as a bullet her bodyguards
formed a human fence around her
to hide the fact that the would-be queen was ill
obas being super-human
were under no circumstances
allowed to be sick

days later
edeleyo died
and today every crown prince
visits her shrine

now tradition has ruled
no woman will reign in benin

the native doctor who ruled benin

he was not born like the others
but leaped from his mother's thigh
a medicine gourd in his left hand

his fame spread throughout the land
and beyond
even before he was crowned king

as the oba
he prepared charms to protect his people

but this oba reigned for centuries
far too long for everyone
to the gods who sent messages saying he'd overstayed his time

he replied
"what can they do to me?"
soon his son wearied of waiting
and sent him gray hairs from his head
to prove he was growing old
and should ascend the throne
but the oba by way of reply
sent coral beads and chalk mixed with salt
and this message for his son
"life is very sweet"

the oba received complaints galore
letting them slide off his skin
like water off a duck's beak
he'd go when he was ready
not a moment before

at long last he was ready to leave
and he wanted to walk into heaven
in style
he was a magician wasn't he?

so he visited his shrine
and asked the spirits to prepare him for his trip
and as his household and volunteers huddled together
to accompany him
he strode into heaven
leaving trusted servants in charge
until his son was crowned

chichi layor

the journey began with great fanfare
from benin they went to the river again
which the oba caused to recede
by chanting a few magic words
and the procession pushed on

soon they were stopped by some short men
carrying pots on their heads
they told the oba to turn back
because humans could not walk into heaven
without angering the gods

the oba turned back
procession and all
emptying their charms
on a river bank
and then
he died with all his retinue

ovia river

ovia was a delectable dame
dark chocolate skin glowed like gold in the sun
eyes were clear come-hither pools
long black hair in braids and beads
she was plump and juicy like a factory uhen

none of the men in ohen was good enough for her
faster than they wooed her she turned them down
and her poor father was going crazy with worry
and growing so thin he was in danger of disappearing
when ovia finally found her man
the king of oyo and no other

now oyo was a long way off
but the king being flush and famous
convinced ovia's father to let her go
so he gave her a pot a parrot and a dog
and told her to use the pot in emergencies

the king of oyo was a virile man
and had a house overflowing with wives
all shapes and sizes and temperaments
the more the merrier is a well-known maxim
heartily adhered to by tribal kings
so ovia was only a drop in the bucket
but she soon swam to the top
and thus became the king's favorite wife
beguiled by ovia's beauty
he couldn't conceal the fact
so the other wives saw seethed and swore
to put the new wife in her proper place

naturally the senior wife was the worst-hit by ovia's charms
she was aging fast and approaching menopause
and was not elated by ovia's looks
for old women are uncomfortable when dry bones are mentioned

the first wife patiently plotted and planned
until she hit upon the perfect scheme
all the king's wives would go snail-hunting by the river
so she got the women together
but poor ovia was misinformed

the wives went down to the river
and the snail-hunt was so successful
everyone had a bag full of snails
except ovia who had no bag
but she had a lovely white cloth
which she treasured with all her heart

senior wife slyly suggested that ovia use her cloth
to carry her own catch
and ovia who had more beauty than brains
carried snails home in her salt-white cloth

of course the cloth was completely ruined
its whiteness now a welter of stains
so first wife whizzed off to see the king
told him ovia suffered from a strange disease

29

and had permanent non-stop periods
first wife advised him to avoid ovia
for his health's sake
and the king obeyed

pining and fretting and craving for his touch
ovia hid herself
embarrased and ashamed
afraid to tell him the truth
lest he disbelieve

then she remembered her father's gifts
the pot would help her if she entered it
so she did
and was instantly turned into water
fast-flowing and clear like her eyes

she flowed home to father in uhen
forever distrustful of females she remained
as she warned her father not to let women
into the secrets of the ovia cult

today ovia is a river and a women no longer
but the gifts from her father are there still
the dog is used as a sacrifice to her
the parrot's feathers are found in her worshippers' head dresses
and the snail in the ovia river

ikpoba river

oba ewuare was a manly man
a welter of wives the oba had
for variety is the sauce of life
and women spice up their masters' lives

now the oba had a favorite wife
called okpese
she was rather plain
but youth was on her side
she was at the helm of the oba's harem

and he hardly even saw his other wives
joined in jealousy
they swore to stop okpese's rule

they paid a medicine man to prepare a spell
for okpese
poor favorite wife
and one eventful evening
royal harem was routinely entertaining
the oba in his palace
when lo and behold
okpese broke wind in a spectacular way
shocking everyone

the spell had worked well
okpese's shame made her shrink
like a punctured balloon
and she told the oba
she was leaving soon
to hibernate in her home town

the oba turned pale
mouth corners sagging
like a tired mattress
as he sputtered his protest

how dare she leave her lord and master
what's become of his harem
then?
soup without salt was unthinkable

but her embarrassment was embedded in her soul
and in spite of him
she stole away in the night

in the morning he sent messengers after her
with a desperate plea that she come right back
but okpese refused to return
and rolled on the ground
weeping wordlessly
until she became a fast-flowing river

ekpenede

oba ehengbuda had only one daughter
called isiuwa
and she married ekpenede
the iyase

naturally ekpenede had many wives
and even more children
the exact number is never mentioned
one counts his children at his own risk
and dares the gods to decimate his descendants

virility was judged by the size of one's male progeny
within wedlock and without
and poor ekpenede had just one son

as if this weren't bad enough
when ekpenede was away at war
his heir had an adulterous affair
with one of the oba's wives

tried by a traditional court
he was found guilty
and executed:
purloining the oba's property
was a heinous crime against the state

ekpenede returned from war
and consumed with crazy shame
killed all his wives
and his household
and then he killed himself
this last an abomination in benin

thereafter
a law was passed
prohibiting the iyase from living near the palace

ise and oba ozolua

ozolua killed a warrior
then took his wife
and made the warrior's only son a sword-bearer

the sword-bearer's name was ise
and he grew up to become
a thorn in the oba's flesh

when ozolua killed ise's mother
hell was let loose
as both men fought ferociously
until ozolua beat a hasty retreat
shinnying up a kolanut tree

ise would have cut down the tree
but it was forbidden to fell kolanut trees
as kola was used to appease the gods

ise waited for ozolua to descend
so that he could finish him off
but the king stayed perched upon the tree
a piteous far-from-regal position
when his former sword-bearer passed by

stunned by the sight of ozolua
the ex-sword-bearer implored ise
to let ozolua come down
and they could settle their differences
through a wrestling match

at his suggestion ozolua shrank
but shame did not permit him to protest
ise however was eager to wrestle
and they did

with succor from the ex-sword-bearer
ozolua threw ise down
beheading him

33

then fearing that his helper would give him away
and tell the people of his cowardice
ozolua sneaked up on his savior
and slew him

now ise is remembered for his manliness

master thief

a skilled thief lived in a village called charm
during the reign of oba esigie
ata was as daring as they come
and well deserved to be called
the king of thieves

they claimed he could steal a child
from its mother's back
and once it was even said he stole a child
from its mother's womb

he put spells on people to make them sleep
while he silently stripped them of their things
like any professional
he took his task most seriously

one day he went to a nearby village to steal
it was sacrifice time
and the village chief and his household were gathered in the courtyard
offering pounded yam and meat to the gods
when the chief espied ata on his pear tree
calmly stealing the fruits
so the chief and his household gave chase

ata leaped from the tree in monkey-like agility
and snatched the sacrificial yam and meat
and fled

the chief had hung his coral beads
all around the pear tree

to keep thieves away
but ata stole the beads as well
when the chief reported the case to the oba
he was blamed for misusing coral beads

one day ata went to the oba with an announcement
he was leaving benin for other lands
with bigger challenges for a master thief

the iyase told him to swallow his boast
and swore that ata could not steal from his house
never one to resist a challenge ata retorted
if the iyase gave him a date
he would rob him then
was a thief ever more fair than that?

before the oba and other chiefs
the iyase gave ata a date seven days hence
and all agreed that if ata was caught
he'd be killed
and if successful he could keep whatever he stole

now the iyase being a medicine man
believed no one could rob him
not even the master thief

ata sent the iyase many reminders
of their robbery rendezvous
ata was confident he could carry it off

then came the appointed day
after breakfast the iyase went to bed
with all his household
so they could stay up at night
to watch for the thief

the gods seemed to be on the iyase's side
for the moon was full
and the stars were bright
the perfect night for outdoor games
who would dare sleep such a night away?

the iyase locked all entrances to his house
and stood guard at the main door
as everyone slowly went to sleep
leaving him with his favorite wife

ata got all his charms together
first he put one in a pot of water
so that a heavy rain drove everybody indoors
then he put another spell on the iyase and his wife
so they began to yawn and fall asleep

when they staggered into bed
ata entered their house
with more magic to stop anyone waking
before he was done
swiftly and silently he stole everything
including the clothes on their backs
as the iyase and his wife lay naked and sleeping
ata turned them around ever so gently
until they lay in opposite directions
then he left the house locking up after him

once home he waited until sunrise
then undid the soporific spell
the iyase and household woke and found
they were naked and the house was bare
so they went whining to the oba

the iyase was reminded of his bet
and the thief was told he could keep his booty
but might take pity on the iyase
so ata divided his booty into two
giving one share to the iyase
and the other to the state
he then promised the oba he'd leave benin
and go stealing in other lands
as a present from his expedition he promised
to bring the oba an entire town
the thief left for the city of ighan
and there his charm enchanted everyone

the chief of ighan took him in with love
and for three years ata did not steal
so the chief trusted him absolutely
teaching his traditions often concealed from strangers
he was even shown the ighan drums
which strangers weren't allowed to touch
only the villagers could beat the drums
in wartime or on the death of a chief

ata advised the chief to send all his subjects
to clear and cultivate farmlands for him
no single soul should stay home
while the chief himself supervised their work
the chief hung on ata's every word
and followed the advice most faithfully

so everyone went out to farm
including the chief and the ex-thief
the blind and the lame were taken along
and the chief went round to check that everyone left

at the farm ata feigned sudden illness
begging that he should be taken home to die
the chief offered to take him home
but he said it was forbidden for the chief to return
so the chief told him where the medicines were kept
and very sadly parted from him

once out of the chief's sight
ata ran back to town
searching for something to steal
but all he saw was the state drum
in the custody of the ighan chief

the people heard drumming
and couldn't believe their ears
for no one had been left at home
when the chief told them about ata
they rushed home weeping
forgetting to take their infirm relatives with them

37

ata hung the drum around his neck
beating it in gay abandon
so the people dressed in dirty work clothes
chased him
crying as if their hearts would burst

with the whole village at his heels
ata ran to benin
and waltzed into the palace
demanding to see the oba at once
it was a matter of urgency

as he beat the ighan drum
the villagers poured into the palace courtyard
and all the palace gates were shut
at the oba's command
so that he could hear ata's case

now the ighan people were all there
including the chief and the infirm
when ata told the oba
he'd kept his promise
and returned with a whole town
and his sweeping arm indicated the ighans

the bini people cheered and cheered
ata was now a national hero
and he gave the oba the ighan drum
today used during festivals
and named after the master thief
the ighan people settled in benin

the greedy hunter

there was once a hunter called long-life
who was greatly distressed for day after day
he failed to find any game in his traps
what kind of hunter was he?

38

feeling suicidal he consulted an oracle
and was told to offer sacrifices
so that all would be well
provided he wasn't greedy

he did as he was told
and went hunting again
this time killing an elephant
a bush pig
and smaller game

heaving the elephant on his head
he put the other game in his bag
and slinging it over his shoulder
started for home

on the way he saw a cricket hole
beside a river
and digging with his big toe
he tried to catch crickets
as well

but the bag containing the smaller game
slipped from his grasp
and as he sought to save the bag
the elephant
and himself
long-life fell into the river

he only just escaped being drowned
but he lost everything
through greed

joromi the wrestler

in a village in benin
lived a fourteen-year-old boy
renowned for his wrestling prowess
his name was joromi

he was like the proverbial cat
whose back never reaches the ground
and no one had succeeding
in throwing him yet

always he sought
to show off his skill
and would gladly wrestle
anything in sight

his parents warned him off a palm tree
growing in their yard
saying the spirits would slay him
if he touched their tree

this warning aroused his curiosity
so he swore to climb the tree
as soon as he found the opportunity
and he did

when his father went to the farm
and his mother to the market
joromi climbed the palm tree

at the top he heard spirits
wrestling below
so he hurried down
to join the fun

with his younger sister hot on his heels
he went to the wrestling ground
and challenged the spirits
to a wrestling match

there were spirits with two heads
three four and five
but the fearless boy felled them
excising their extra heads

finally only one spirit king was left
this one had seven horrendous heads

and just the sight of him would scare any fourteen-year-old
but not joromi
he would wrestle immediately
against his sister's wish

what teenager ever listens to his sister?
joromi wrestled with the spirit king
this way and that
with expert skill
but the king of spirits killed him
in the end

then the spirit went to fetch water
firewood and food ingredients
for turning joromi into a tasty meal
he left a lame man
and a blind man
to guard the boy's body
until his return

soon as he left
the sensible sister squeezed liquid from magic leaves
into joromi's eyes and ears
bringing him back to life
and as they were escaping
the spirit returned
and gave chase

joromi was at the door to his home
when the spirit king caught up with him
and as joromi went through
the spirit scratched his back
with long long nails

the resultant mark
is the depression in our backs

eneka

at the annual festival of the oba of benin
he was dressed in his dandy state robe
the cynosure for everyone

thousands of spectators thronged the city
among them eneka's mama
with him strapped securely to her back
when the baby began to cry
the frantic mom fought her way out of the crowd

finding herself beside a high wall
she touched it and a door opened
leading into passage after passage
till she got lost in the labyrinth

at last she came to a garden of weeds
and rested awhile
letting eneka run free
finding another door
that led to the back of the palace
she hurried home
abandoning the oba festival and all
unaware as she was
that the garden was enchanted
and her child by extension
an enchanted child

henceforth he became handsome and strong
as the only son of a poor man
who lived in uzebu
a province under the chief ezomo

now a handsome young man
eneka prepared to take part in the oba's annual festival
in benin city

the oba was decked out in his famous robe of coral beads
as all the chiefs in his empire

paid homage and danced before him
to the rhythm of drums and trumpets

at some point each chief in turn
would dance before the oba
flourishing a sword
first flinging it into the air
and catching it by the hilt
then dipping the point before the oba
as the chief knelt in homage
offering special gifts
to the stern-faced oba

soon it was the turn of the ezomo
chief of uzebu province
where eneka lived
now the ezomo flung his sword in the air
and quick as a bullet
without warning
eneka leaped and caught the sword
then fled

for a moment
the crowd was stunned
then recovering their composure
gave chase

although eneka dropped the sword
his pursuers followed him to uzebu
until they reached his father's house
thus trapping him
as they moved in for the kill
eneka ordered all to stand still
and they did
sheepishly
and helplessly
then they wandered off in different directions

the news spread all over the empire
elevating eneka
in the eyes of all

at the yearly wrestling contest
in the oba's palace
champions from all over the land
came to wrestle in benin city
but the oba's champions were indomitable

the greatest of all was igbadaken
a colossus
a fearsome sight

the match began
and the ezomo's wrestlers lost
one by one
so that the ezomo was suffused with shame
as he watched igbadaken flaunting his metallic muscles

no wrestler himself
eneka shared the ezomo's shame
and didn't want the uzebu team disgraced
so all of a sudden
he darted into the arena
challenging the awesome igbadaken

you could have heard a leaf drop
in the silence of the spectators
and then igbadaken laughed
his shoulders heaving

you gnat he bellowed
do you wish to die?

the jeers of the oba's followers
merely spurred eneka on
and he circled round the champ
in slow motion
waiting for a chance to make his move

this went on for minutes
and then the hulk seized eneka by the waist
throwing him in the air

like a cat he landed on his feet
then seized the unsuspecting igbadaken
and dashed him to the ground

the champion collapsed like a sack of rice

the crowd went wild with surprise
as eneka was borne shoulder high to uzebu
grinning from ear to ear
the ezomo make eneka a senior servant
and gave one of his daughters in marriage
to him

fame went to eneka's head
and he saw all work
as infradig
when the ezomo advised him against loafing
he decided to be a hunter

getting his traps together
he sallied forth into the forest
and each time a trap caught an animal
he let it go

one day he watched as a woman stole a rabbit

from one of his traps
he looked again and saw it was
one of the oba's wives
any man who spoke to them
was instantly beheaded

forgetting this in a fit of fury
eneka slapped the oba's wife
the oba forgave eneka his crime
on account of his ezomo's pleas
but warned eneka to avoid the palace
and not hunt near it again

giving up hunting altogether
he led the life of a lounger

once more
when the ezomo chided him
he left uzebu for benin city

as he lolled around
he came to a stream
beside the oba's palace
and climbed up a nearby tree

when some women came bathing in the stream
he recognized them as the oba's wives
and froze in fear
for to see an oba's wife bathing
was to die
for sure
so eneka sat deathly still in the tree
till one woman looked up
saw him and screamed
then they all grabbed their clothes
and fled

this time the oba did not forgive
but condemned eneka to death
he would be sacrificed in a festival
in a few days' time
meanwhile he was locked in a gloomy cell

hungry and hopeless he wished to die
and began to sing very doleful tunes
when a rat came through the mud ceiling
and addressed him thus:

remember me
animal lover?
i'm the friend you freed from your trap

eneka simply stared in shock
at the speaking rat
then found his tongue and admitted
to freeing more animals than he could remember

waving that aside the rat went on
to assure eneka he would be saved
by animals he'd freed in the past
then the rat went to rally other beasts

on the day of the festival
the oba's first daughter came of age
and the oba celebrated in style
surrounded by his subjects from all over benin

sounds of pomp reached eneka
in his lonely cell
as he recalled the rat's promise
a trifle skeptically

the oba's daughter was bathing in a private garden
in readiness for her special ceremony
when a vicious viper bit her ankle
acting on orders from eneka's rat

minutes later the princess was dead

when the oba heard the sad news
he ended the festival abruptly
ordering the most famous witch doctors in the empire
to resuscitate his beloved daughter
but it was all of no avail

as instructed by the rat
eneka started to sing self-confidently
about his ability to revive the princess
so that the oba was duly informed
and ordered that eneka be brought to him

out of malice
igbadaken asked the oba to ignore
eneka's crazy claim
but the oba distraught and desperate
offered eneka his freedom
if only he could bring the princess back to life

a dirty and dishevelled eneka went to work
fathering herbs from the princess' garden
and acting on the animals' instructions
he revived the princess in a matter of minutes
then led her by the hand to her father

overjoyed the oba ordered that the festival go on
and gave eneka a special seat of honor
the oba's daughter had fallen in love with eneka
and she asked her father if she could marry him

the oba gladly gave his consent to the marriage
and made eneka a special chief

omofoma and adese

in a town near benin city
lived a young farmer called omofoma

on the other side of town
lived three delectable damsels
and omofoma planned to marry all three

when the first one came of age
he asked for her hand
and got it
then set a wedding date
but she died before the wedding
unexpectedly

omofoma mourned for a time
then the second girl came of age
and he asked for her hand
successfully
but she drowned in a stream
on the wedding day

grief-stricken omofoma would commit suicide
but friends saved and consoled him
reminding him of the third maiden

she came of age
and he asked for her hand
but planned to have the wedding
without publicity
on the wedding day
she took ill and died

this time omofoma went wild with grief
and would not bathe
or comb his hair
finally he wandered off to benin city

the oba of benin was steeped in sorrow
for his eldest son was in the throes of death

prince imadasun had gone hunting one night
when a nameless beast
part elephant
part bull
attacked the prince and his troupe
goring him gravely

the oba consulted a wise old woman
who said that a bell around the beast's neck
could cure the prince
if he used it as a cup

straight away the oba sent hordes of servants
to capture the beast
but they lost their lives
instead

the oba's despair knew no bounds
and princess adese began to sicken
she was imadasun's twin sister
and might die with him

omofoma was about to enter benin city
when he saw an old lady hobbling along
a heavy bundle of firewood upon her head
omofoma was moved to tears

and relieved her of her heavy load
which he carried all the way to her home

the etchings on her face were effaced by gratitude
and she pledged to procure a wife for him
if only he stayed a few days with her
so he did

the wizened woman visited the spirit world
returning with the remedy to omofoma's plight
if he did exactly as he was told
he would marry princess adese

omofoma split his sides with laughter

slowly the old woman subdued his skepticism
and told him in detail what he had to do
first tie a piece of wood to a long string
to obtain a make-shift musical instrument
now clean up completely
then go to the oba with a plum proposal
to cure the dying prince
and marry his twin sister

omofoma did as he was told
going into the forest
with the musical instrument
his only weapon

the grotesque animal came growling at him
but he pacified it by whirling the wood at the end of a string
producing an eerie high-pitched hum
then he led the subdued beast away
to a cross-roads where a man stood guard

delighted to have found the runaway beast
the guard took its chain from omofoma
telling him to come to the spirit world
for a rousing reward

acting on instructions he declined the guard's offer

and asked for the bell around the beast's neck
gladly the guard gave the bell to him
and omofoma rushed back to the city
all the way to the oba's palace

the oba and adese were jubilant
and the bell was promptly filled with water
from which the ailing imadasun drank

he recovered some days later
and omofoma got his reward
the oba gave him adese's hand in marriage
and plenty of presents besides
but omofoma did not forget his friend
he took the old woman back to his home town
where he lived happily with princess adese

much ado about a woman

two rival towns
ehor and iruele
were sometimes enemies
sometimes friends

the leader of iruele
was ovbioghumu
and the leader of ehor
okosun

one day ovbioghumu visited okosun
but okosun's winsome wife ibo
failed to have a meal waiting
disgraced
okosun wanted to whip her
but ovbioghumu pleaded with him to pardon her
and a guest's wish is always granted

when his guest left
okosun cut off ibo's hair

and made her sit under the blazing sun
ordering her not to speak to anyone

for hours
she sat in the sun
until ovbioghumu's servant saw her
and raced to iruele with his report

ovbioghumu flew off the handle
okosun had reneged on his promise to pardon ibo
so ovbioghumu ordered his servant to go to ehor
and bring the hapless ibo to iruele

okosun could not believe that ibo
had dared to disappear
and he searched everywhere for her
in vain

when he heard she was living with ovbioghumu in iruele
he sent a trusted servant to ascertain if it was true
atuke climbed a pear tree beside ovbioghumu's house
and saw ovbioghumu lying with ibo

dismayed
atuke came down from the tree
and accused ovbioghumu of wife stealing
the iruele leader's response was to cut off the servant's ears
immerse him in a giant pot of poison
and send him back to okosun in ehor
where the servant slumped and died after giving his report

the people of ehor declared war against iruele
and massacred many of the iruele warriors

retaliating
ovbioghumu bribed one of okosun's slaves
and together they slaughtered a stolen cow
then made it seem as if okosun was the thief

destroyed by the false charges

okosun committed suicide
his friend esegbe became the new leader of ehor

confident of victory now that okosun was dead
ovbioghumu sent his servant to esegbe
demanding the ehor people's capitulation
but esegbe recalling how okosun's servant was treated
lopped off the ears and arms of ovbioghumu's courier
then sent him back to iruele to die

now ehor and iruele waged total war against each other
devastation was the name of the game
until they came to their senses
and called for a truce
to enable their elders to resolve the conflict
finally both towns agreed there'd be no more war

and from then on
ehor and iruele became known for their friendship

the fighter

a long time ago
there was a man who had three sons
okougbo the farmer
okohue the hunter
and okodan the fighter

the two older ones worked hard for a living
while the third son did nothing but fight
anyone in sight
robbing his victims
simultaneously

in vain his brothers tried
to get okodan to go straight

one day he met the oba's eldest son
and dared him to a fight

when the prince put up a stout defense
okodan bashed his head with a club
and moments later
the prince was dead

now murder in the land was anathema
but killing the oba's son was unthinkable
so okodan hastily hid the corpse
and conceived a way to conceal his crime

he asked okohue if he could go hunting with him
and pray what path would he take the next day?
delighted that the fighter was ready to go straight
okohue gave him the details of the next day's hunt
but later in the day
okodan returned to say
he'd be unable to be at their rendezvous
and could they go hunting some other time?

the next day okohue went hunting alone
and saw a big animal sleeping behind a bush
he skillfully gunned it down
then found it was the oba's eldest son

horrified okohue beat a hasty retreat
and once home he locked himself in

soon okodan came calling on his brother
and finding the hunter unusually jumpy
he convinced okohue to confide in him

when okohue told him he'd shot the oba's son
okodan offered to get him out of trouble
if the hunter would always provide him with meat
at this point okohue would have done anything

the fighter went to his brother the farmer
with a request that okougbo teach him to farm
they arranged to go farming the following day
but okodan later changed his mind

54

okougbo went to his farm along
and saw someone trying to steal his yams
so he took a big stick and hit the thief over the head
when the figure rolled over and lay deathly still
the farmer saw it was the oba's eldest son

aghast okougbo ran all the way home
and when he got there okodan was waiting
the fighter noticed his brother's distress
and his concern earned him the role of confidant

when okougbo told him he'd killed the oba's son
the fighter waved his brother's fright aside
and pledged to put things right at once
if okougbo would always provide him with yams

quickly the farmer accepted the deal
so okodan removed the body from the farm

the guards at the palace had fallen asleep
when the oba woke in the middle of the night
he saw a dark figure crouching in a corner
and grabbing a nearby bronze statuette
he brought it down heavily on the burglar's head

the intruder was dead without a doubt
and when the oba lit a hurricane lamp
he realized he had killed his eldest son

horrified and heart-broken
the oba hid the corpse in an inner room
and in the morning would see no one

the chiefs thought his behavior strange
and as palace guards gathered in groups to gossip
okodan slipped into the oba's room

the fighter asked the oba what the reason was
for not meeting with the chiefs as he always did
the oba saw sincerity in the fighter's face

and compassion in his whole demeanor
so he poured his troubles into okodan's ear

okodan told the oba to chin up
the fighter could get him out of the mess
for that the oba promised a rich reward

okodan went to the room where the corpse lay
and placing charms on the dead man's clothes
he powdered the lifeless face
lit a fire beneath the body
then killed some chickens and hung them around a wooden image

after okodan told him what to say
the oba called in his chiefs
and sadly told them the following story

the reason he'd retired to his private room
was because his eldest son had been ill
and thought the oba had smeared him with oil
sacrificed animals to the gods
and remained with him all night and day
the prince had passed away

the chiefs swallowed the credible tale
and conveyed their condolences to the oba
who kept his word
and rewarded okodan by making him a chief
the ogiagbanaku
and even today the people of that town
are renowned for their great cunning

the unlucky one

in a village near benin city
a poor farmer called omoike lived with his two sons
oboika and omoegbebe

omoegbebe means unlucky one
for his mother died having him

and months later
his father passed away

fearful of the ill luck that omoegbebe brought
on one in the village would have the two boys
so oboika a mere seven-year-old
raised his little brother with proceeds from a small farm
and they both grew up healthy and strong

omoegbebe soon wanted his own farm
and found in the forest
an old burial ground
which he cleared in preparation for sowing crops
in defiance of village traditions and laws

he borrowed okra seeds which he sowed on the land

and faster than it takes to say thank you
the plants reached remarkable size
but when he went to harvest them
antelopes had eaten the entire crop

nothing daunted he began all over again
sowing corn this time around
the corn did incredibly well
but the villagers would not tough any crop grown on a burial ground

when omorgbebe went to reap his corn
wild birds had destroyed most of it
reining in his rage
he tried to trap the birds
but they escaped unexpectedly
save for one which struggled in his grip
then flew away leaving its head in his hand

sadly he surveyed the ruins of his farm
and putting the bird's head in his shoulder bag
began to trudge home
en route he met the oba's messengers
who questioned his queasy look
so he recounted his strange tale

to buttress his story he put his hand in his bag
and pulled out the bird's head
which in a split second became a bull's head
and the messengers mauled omoegbebe

he could not explain how he got the bull's head
and the oba's cow had just been stolen
so omoegbebe was branded as a thief
and taken immediately to see the oba of benin

the oba ruled that omoegbebe be sacrificed
whenever a suitable occasion arose
and until then he was to act as a servant
to one of the oba's many wives

one day the oba's wife gave omoegbebe a piece of yam
in recognition of his splendid services
happily he put the yam down on the kitchen floor
then went to fetch a knife to cut up the yam
when he returned a goat had eaten it all
so he threw the knife at the hungry goat
but missed
and broke the knife in two

now the knife belonged to the oba's wife
and she ordered omoegbebe to mend it at once
so he went to the village blacksmith
who offered to mend it for free

omoegbebe offered to work the bellows
and by sheer accident set the smithy on fire
the king blacksmith did not scold the bungler
but sought his help in getting thatch for the roof
ever eager to work omoegbebe scaled a palm tree
and began to cut down branches singing gaily

about an hour later he heard shouting down below
a huge crowd had gathered and was calling to him
so he looked down and saw a dead man lying there
with a fresh palm frond sticking out of his head
omoegbebe looked again and saw it was one of the oba's sons

this was all he needed to make his misery complete
he discarded his climbing ropes
and hurtled headlong from the top of the tree
the crowd dispersed in various directions
but the would-be suicide was unsuccessful
for he somersaulted and landed on his feet
surprised to be safe

now the angry crowd took him to the oba
who though devastated by the death of his son
could not sentence omoegbebe twice to death
he had to wait until he could be sacrificed
so he was ordered to serve another one of the oba's wives

omoegbebe began to hunt small game
while serving the oba's wife satisfactorily
one day he found a farm of yams in the forest
and after checking that the coast was clear
began to dig up the yummy yams

he was surprised by a hand on his back
it was the great chief iyasele
the owner of the farm
omoegbebe lied through his teeth
and said he'd been hunting rabbits

unimpressed
the iyasele took omoegbebe to the oba
and the thief denied having designs on the yams
claiming he'd been digging for rabbits

in an attempt to debunk omoegbebe's claim
the iyasele vowed that if his accusation was disproved
he would give half of his possessions to omoegbebe
if the oba would repeal his death sentence
but the iyasele asked that omoegbebe be killed
if he was found to be digging up yams

the oba granted the iyasele's request
and sent witnesses with both men to the iyasele's farm

where the onus was on omoegbebe to produce a rabbit

already sentenced to death omoegbebe was unruffled
and flet that he had nothing to lose
so he went with the witnesses and the iyasele to the farm
and continued digging from where he'd left off

mystifying everyone including himself
omoegbebe pulled a rabbit out of the hole

trapped by his own pledge was the iyasele
compelled to give half of his property to omoegbebe
who was also granted a state pardon

to top it off the oba made him a chief
so omoegbebe returned to his little village
to share his fortune with his older brother
now his luck had completely changed
he and his brother became rich and famous

otolo

in a town called ikhin
a poor woman once lived
who was despised by everyone
for she was childless
and no worse fate could befall a woman

at long last the gods blessed her
with a baby boy
whom she named otolo

he was a child like no other
for he crawled at three months
walked at six
and talked at nine
when he was one year
he seemed to be twelve
then at two
he was a full-grown man

he went to see a wrestling match
one day
and leaped into the ring
determined to demonstrate how really to wrestle

at first
no one dared take on the two-year-old
for you could see with half an eye
his superior strength

a daredevil twenty-year-old
walked toward otolo
who grabbed then lifted him high in the air
and threw him
the young man rolled over
like wheels on a moving cart

other wrestlers accepted otolo's challenge
and all without exception
were thrown
so that otolo became known
as the strong man of ikhin
and no one taunted his mother
anymore

one day otolo entered
an archery contest
where the rule was that the winner
took two arrows from the losers
when otolo lost all his arrows
he knocked down the winners
and retrieved his arrows
otolo bought a dog
which he took hunting with him
but when the dog stole otolo's meat
he told his mother
she must sell the dog

the woman went to the market
but no one wanted to buy the dog

then just as she was about to leave
a tall young man swaggered to her stall

haughtily he introduced himself
as omoweme of erara

then he seized the dog
and stalked out of the market

when otolo's mother reported the robbery
to her son
he set out to subdue
the swashbuckling stranger

omoweme was feared in erara town
he had been in many wars
and collected human skulls

no one dared say his name aloud
for his house was painted blood-red
when a frightened man pointed it out from a distance
otolo strode to omoweme's house

omoweme was out
but otolo calmly waited for the warrior to return
when omoweme came
the dog at his heels
otolo retrieved his dog
and marched to the door

like a lightning streak
omoweme struck
and the two men exchanged
the most brutal blows

a crowd gathered
but didn't dare interfere
in the fight between giants
so they fought on and on
until they both collapsed

and died
in the spirit world they still fought
until they were reported to baba
king of the spirit world

he listened to both men
and sentenced omoweme to the spirit world
forever
but otolo who had been provoked
was allowed to return to the world
stripped of his super-human strength

in erara they were about to bury both men
when otolo's body moved
and he came back to life
but omoweme was undoubtedly dead

otolo was now a normal man
with no recollection of his former strength
or the famous fight with omoweme
though his mother often spoke of it
as mothers are wont to do
otolo led a very happy life

ORACLES DON'T LIE

Tales from Yorubaland

AUTHOR'S NOTES

The Yoruba say they have 401 orisha or divinities. The orisha are seen as part-manifestations of Olodumare, the supreme God.

Orisha nla, or Obatala, is the most senior of the orisha. The color white is associated with him: white temple, white clothes, white chalk and white beads. This symbolizes purity. *Oje* is a white metal considered sacred by Obatala's priests who wear wristlets of *oje*. Obatala is known as the creator of men, but in traditional myth, he also takes other form, such as the mother of King Shango, or an old man, a friend of Shango's.

Orunmila is the oracle-divinity famed for his foreknowledge and wisdom. The Ifa system of divination is a part of the cult of Orunmila. The Yorubas have complete faith in Ifa who is consulted for guidance before any action is ever taken. Orunmila is believed to be a great doctor and the ifa priests claim that Osanyin is the doctor's divinity and orunmila's younger brother. The shrine of Orunmila is often in the home. Emblems are mainly sixteen palm-nuts in a bowl, some pieces of elephant tusk and cowries. The babalawo, or priest, wears strings of beads on his wrist, holds a divining rod made from elephant tusk in one hand and a switch made from animal skin in the other.

Osanyin is the divinity associated with the knowledge of herbs.

Eshu represents the unpredictable element of fate. He is dreaded by the Yorubas because he is a mischief-maker and is associated with everything evil.

Yemanja is often considered the senior of all river goddesses, the water of life.

Ogun is one of the earliest divinities to be created, the god of iron and steel, of war and warriors. He is wild and ferocious.

Sakpata is the god of suffering who teaches his followers to cope with misfortune. Sakpata is the Fon name for Shopona.

Shopona is the god of smallpox, "the destruction that wasteth at noonday." He is a dread to the Yorubas and is thought to be armed with poisonous arrows and small gourds. The Yorubas use small gourds to keep curative and preventive medicine and also poison. They believe that Shopona pubishes the wicked in the society.

Oro is a secret cult concerned with worship of the dead.

In the past the *Aremo* (oldest prince) shared the king's reign but had to die with him too. Direct father-to-son succession has been ruled out in all Yorubaland. On a king's death, the succession passes to another royal house.

A Yoruba greeting says, "May your secret not be discovered" and that is why it is considered important not to reveal someone's secret (see poems about Otin on p. 45 and about Yemanja on p.47.)

There is a Yoruba proverb: "You are a king and you still want to make magic. Do you want to become God?" (See poem about Orisha Oko on page 25.)

The Yorubas believe that man's character is most important and it is what Olodumare judges. The Yoruba word *Iwa* means "good character"; *Iwa* is also the name of Orunmila's wife, and the mother of many children.

Women are excluded from the Oro and Egungun secret cults into which some men are initiated. However, the women are allowed to bring food offerings to the shrine during certain rituals.

There are shrines all over Yorubaland. Certain spirits are thought to reside in the *iroko* (African teak) and egungun (silk cotton) trees. Rivers, lakes and streams are always associated with spirits and every body of water is believed to have an "owner."

YORUBALAND

EDITOR'S NOTES

When Nigeria became independent in 1960, it was comprised of a federation of three distinct groups, although there were many smaller tribes in the area. The Northern Region was dominated by the Hausa, who were Muslims, ruled by emirs. The Eastern was primarily Edo, ruled by tribal chiefs. The Western Region was Yoruba, ruled by kings. Yoruba is among the largest ethnic groups in West Africa.

An old tradition says that the founding ancestor, Oduduwa, came from the east, possibly Sudan. Among the various Yoruban kingdoms, the first sizeable one was empire of Oyo, which at its height, exceeded its eastern neighbor, the Ibo Kingdom of Benin, in size and might. Oyo rose in the late 16th century following an invasion by their northern neighbors, the Nupe, who drove the king, or alafin, into exile. When Alafin Orompoto returned, he came with 1,000 mounted warriors and set about organizing the kingdom into a tight system of guards, the Esho; tribute collectors, the Ilau; the hereditary chiefs, the Oyomesi, and sub-chiefs which made for a strong kingdom for more than 200 years. The towns are ruled by members of the Ogboni, the most influential local citizens.

Yorubans were--and are--industrious, having manufacturing guilds and establishing trade routes north to the Sahara and south to the Gold Coast. Among their products were cloth and beads.

In the late 18th centhury, in an Islamic jihad, Fulani invaded the Oyo empire and occupied its northern territories. With the kingdom in disarray, slavers moved into Yorubaland, which supplied most of the slaves exported by Dahomey and various Europeans, who sold them in Cuba and Brazil. The export of slaves continued until the mid-19th century.

The population is highly urbanized, with the Yoruban city of Idaban being the largest totally African city south of the Sahara. The Yorubas call their holy city Ife.

The Yoruba still practice ritualistic death of the king. Ancient kings were usually deified after death.

oduduwa

king lamurudu ruled mecca
another mecca
not the place of pilgrimage

one day the muslims came
bearing the message of islam to the people
who destroyed their idols
embracing islam with wide-open arms

now the king had a son called oduduwa
a fiery infidel
who loathed the muslims
and swore to stop them spreading their religion in his town

he befriended asara the idol-carver
and together they placed idols in the city mosque
then tricked the people into praying to the idols

one day they'd get even

the idol-carver had a son called braimoh
who helped to sell his father's idols on the streets
but unknown to his father
he accepted the teachings of islam

still he had to hawk idols for his father
and as he stalked the streets
he cried
"false gods for sale
false gods for sale"

his furious father punished him
but a defiant braimoh vowed to destroy all idols someday

that day came during the yearly festival of the gods
when all the men in mecca went hunting for three days

feigning illness
braimoh stayed behind
alone

axe in hand
he marched into the mosque
and hacked the idols into teeny tiny bits
he left the head idol untouched
with the axe hung on it as a signature
then went away as pleased as punch

three days later the men returned to town
and went to the mosque to worship their idols
but they found none standing except one
braimoh's axe told the whole wild story
so they queried him

he cockily countered
"why ask me?
ask the ugly idol there or can't he
speak?"

replied his astonished accusers
"ask an idol?
can an idol speak?"

braimoh's salvo was swift
"pathetic pin-heads
why worship something which cannot
speak?"

enraged
they decreed his death

as they prepared to incinerate him
other muslims rushed to his rescue
and fierce fighting broke out
'tween the muslims and the pagans
and lamurudu the king was killed

now that their leader was no more

the pagans fled the town in fear
ditto for oduduwa and two of his brothers
the brothers moved west and founded gogobiri and kukawa
                    kingdoms in hausaland
while oduduwa and company went east

for days they plodded on
thru arid and antagonistic lands
soldiering on
till they spotted an oasis
where the grass was green
and lush farms lured
oduduwa and co

at the sight of the strangers
the resident farmers fled
but oduduwa's men trapped one
and got him to reveal the name of his settlement
and the name of his tribe

ife was the town
igbo the tribe
replied the farmer
then he was ordered to take them to ife

after ninety drawn-out difficult days
they arrived in ife
to find the houses were deserted
so oduduwa and his men
who seized a copy of the koran from them
and called it *edi*
meaning
"something tied up"
they kept it in a sacred spot in ife
where it's still worshipped today

in ife oduduwa became a mighty king
progenitor-general of the yorubas

but the igbos were hiding in the bushes
and biding their time

chichi layor

moremi's sacrifice

moremi was married to an ancient hero of ile-ife
and her only son was called oluorogbo

no dumb blonde
moremi had beauty
brains
virtue
and black hair

now ife was frequently raided by the igbos
who plundered goods
women and kids

this feud went way back to oduduwa's days

for years
the ife people felt they'd been cursed by the gods
believing that the igboswere no mere mortals
for in truth they were an awesome sight

fully clothed in grass
they looked like creatures from outer space

pretty moremi was driven by patriotic zeal
to free her people from the igbos' hold
so she went to a stream called esinmirin
and invoked the resident deity
vowing that if she succeeded in her mission
she'd give to the god her most precious possession
and if she failed
well she'd only die once

she planned to get close to the igbos
then conquer them
so she let them capture her in their next raid
and owing to her breathtaking beauty
she was given to the king as a special gift
living among them like one of their own

she sussed them out
saw they were ordinary men who covered themselves in grass
so they seemed terrifying and extra-terrestrial
her husband the king demystified them for her
"if you set upon them with lighted torches
they will scatter like weeds"

one day moremi escaped
returning to her homeland with what she'd learned
and the igbos' next raid was routed by the ife people
who attacked the igbos with flaming torches
so that the e-ts in their grass robes went up in smoke

ife liberated
moremi scurried to the stream with offerings of rams and goats
which the god turned down
next she offered a bullock
and still the god said no
then the priests told her
the god demanded
her only son

her blood ran cold
but she'd pledged her most precious possession
hadn't she?
and a pledge was a pledge
so she sacrificed oluorogbo
her only son

they say oluorogbo regained his life
rose into heaven with a rope
and will return someday

sixteen sacred palm-nuts

in the city of ife
lived ifa
a wild-eyed beggar
who come rain or shine
sought alms in the streets

chichi layor

he looked like a loony
and people gave him corn *akara** and cowrie shells
so he would go away

later they tired of giving him alms
and they began to call him names
like lazybones
and crazy man
so that hungry and weary he retired to the bush
praying night and day to the gods for help

one day during prayer he had a dream
in which a man addressed him thus:
"ifa
your prayer has been heard
and i am sent from heaven to give you secret knowledge
that will make you rich
and sought-after by everyone"

the man showed ifa sixteen palm-nuts
the sixteen spirits that controlled men's fate
the first and last were the most important ones
he taught ifa to use the sixteen nuts
to solve any problem that faced him
then the strange man tied a string round ifa's wrist
to remind him of the knowledge he'd received
and the man vanished like smoke

ifa awoke in a mystified state
saw the string and palm nuts
and realized he'd been blessed
he practiced with the palm-nuts
casting them on the ground like dice
studying the different formations
till versed in divination and problem-solving
he could find all he needed
and no longer had to beg

the people were puzzled
when he disappeared from the streets
and wondering what had become of him

they went to his hut
only to find him well-dressed and well-fed

cool as a groom entering the bridal room
ifa asked the people in
offering to answer any questions put to him
and he did

they left his hut
confounded
the poor crazed man was now clever!

as word went round
the nobles and the plebs all scuttled off to seek ifa's help
sickness, war, more
he answered their questions
and grew rich from their gifts

he was called orunmila
the god of wisdom
whose special initiates called *babalawos**
were taught to use the sixteen palm-nuts
and guard the knowledge
only handing it down to other ifa priests

when he died
ifa became the chief oracle
whose priests meet secretly in a forest
today

---

* *akara* - fried beancakes
* *babalawos* - fathers of secrets

and the gods were angry

olodumare the supreme god of the yorubas
loved a lesser god called orunmile
whom he sent down to earth to restore order
whenever the need arose

orunmila lived in ife
at a time when gods lived among men
a furious famine hit ife
and starvation hovered on the horizon
so the elders sought orunmila's help

he consulted the oracle
and was told to offer sacrifices to the angry gods:
two hundred grass-cutters
two hundred goats
two hundred hens
and two hundred of everything in the land

horrified by the huge numbers
the elders disbelieved orunmila
who consulted the gods again

olodumare ordered him to return to heaven
before ife was annihilated
for the people had disregarded orunmila's advice
and for that they'd be chastised

orunmila hooked a rope to the sky
and hurried into heaven

soon as he left
the sky grew dark
and an eerie stillness swooped down
you could have heard a feather drop
and as the wind howled
lightning shot across the sky
thunder roared like a lion with a toothache
and the rain came tumbling down
the people were happy as they envisioned a rich harvest
resulting from the heavy rain
but they became afraid
when the rain swelled rivers
flooded houses
toppled trees
rushed on relentlessly
and drowned everyone

finally the rain stopped
and the sun peeped out
nothing remained of ife
but a solitary coconut tree

the gods in heaven felt pangs of remorse
and sent orunmila to recreate ife

descending his magic rope
he surveyed the bleak and lifeless land
and tried to see where he could begin

he saw the top of a coconut tree above the flood
and surprised to see something had survived
he climbed atop the coconut tree
and reconstructed ife

henceforth
he was known as agbonniregun
or the coconut tree that the sun god climbed

let there be land

when all the *orisha** were created in heaven
oduduwa went to orunmila for oracular counsel
orunmila told him to find a five-toed hen
five chameleons
and five hundred chains

oduduwa did as he was told
then returned to orunmila who prepared a sacrifice
sprinkled wood ash on it
and told oduduwa to take it with him

next oduduwa went to olodumare
who gave him some sand tied in a cloth

when the orisha arrived in the world
all they found was water
water water everywhere and not a spot of land

so they all returned to heaven except oduduwa

he hooked the chains of orunmila into heaven
and climbed down into the world
next he put the sand on the water and it spread and became earth
then he placed the chameleons on the sand
they walked warily testing the ground which proved solid
chameleons still walk that way today

oduduwa now put the hen on the sand
tested the ground with one foot
saw that it was firm
then he came down
unhooked the chains from heaven
and put them at idio near ife
in a place now called the house of oduduwa

aje also known as wealth came down from heaven
to live with oduduwa on earth
and shower him with riches

ogun and obatala bowed down before him
and one by one all the orisha emerged
although orisha-nla is his eldest brother
oduduwa's bravery propelled him into pre-eminence

---

* _orisha_ - divinity/divinities

the sun

agbeji ogbodoso said when the busn fowl awoke
he was sad to see the beanstalk had exceeded his reach

agbeji consulted the oracle for the owner of the forest
and told him to sacrifice lest the iroko tree in his back yard fall
                                        upon him
but the owner of the forest refused to heed this advice
and the iroko tree did fall tho it hung in the air like a crazy
                                        parachute

when the owner called in the woodcarver to cut up the tree
along came obatala the creator of man
and turned the tree into the sacred white metal called *oje*
then he summoned his servant called you-don't-hear-what-i-say
and told him to take the *oje* to the blacksmith in heaven
who would sculpt a fancy pot and boat

thus did you-don't-hear-what-i-say become the driver of the sun
from heaven to earth and back again in one day

the sun's hometown is iwonran
but obatala ordered him to shine on the people every day

the moon

yorubas believe the moon has two unequal sides
the fat side hidden in heaven
and the thin side shown to us down here

ajalorun the spirit of heaven gave birth to the moon
elaparo the rainbow consulted ifa oracle for the moon
and told her to offer sacrifices for her peace of mind
but the moon refused

olodumare then summoned the moon and said
"behold i am your maker
i created you before i gave you to ajalorun who bore you
now i command you to spend fifteen days in heaven
and fifteen days on earth
and for fifteen days i will create men and trees"

olodumare then decreed
henceforth the moon would have no peace of mind
and ifa mocked the moon saying
"you did not sacrifice and so you will not rest
fifteen days here
fifteen days there"

okanbi the brave

in a distant land lived king okikisi
who was skilled in magic
of the white kind
his only child was called okanbi
meaning "an only child"

okanbi didn't know the meaning of fear
and would try anything at least once
adventure was his middle name
he climbed rocks
waded in streams
and shinnied up trees
while his poor father worried himself sick

now the land was in danger
its fertility had fled
and food was as scarce as eels' feet
so kind okikisi summoned all the wise men to his court
where they sought a solution to the problem of starvation

decision: find a fertile place and settle there

fifteen men were chosen to go searching
and adventure-loving okanbi would follow them
but the king fearing for his son's safety
put his foot down and said no

okanbi begged his father on bended knee
to let him go
even if he was an only child
and sole successor to the king
he could charm the birds from the tree
with his silver tongue
and he persuaded the king to let him go on the precarious trip

sixteen men now set out to seek a new settlement
among them two trusted servants of the king
tetu and okinkin the king's trumpeter

the king gave his two two priceless presents
a piece of black cloth and a cock
then told the trumpeter that in the face of danger
he should blow his trumpet

so that okanbi would untie the piece of cloth
and help would come
the king told the trumpeter to look after the cock
for it would help them in its turn

the men ventured into the forest where
monstrous trees touching the sky
let no light thru
as the undergrowth grabbed their legs
and stymied their movement
so that they found little to eat
and much to fear

like howling hyenas
growling lions
slithering snakes
screeching owls
and unidentified sounds at night

still the sixteen pressed on

several days later
they reached a wide river
and a dilemma:
go back thru the forbidding forest
or cross the river so deep and wide

they were between the devil and the deep blue sea

okanbi spoke first
"brothers
 we're a long long way from home
we made it thru the forest
we'll make it thru the river for sure
if we return home now

we'll be called cowards
but if we brave it thru the water
we'll become heroes
and our story will be sung on moonlit nights
and brothers if we die
we die like men!"

okanbi's pep talk propelled them straight
into the river
with the sun overhead
and the heat intense
you could poach an egg in the river
and have a sauna in the stifling air
as they waded thru the water
the men grew weary and silent
afraid of the clouds that hung in the air

they dreaded drowning in the river
if the storm broke
and while some invoked the gods
others cursed okanbi
because he'd convinced them to cross the river

okanbi kept his cool
in the heat of the abuse
for he believed they would survive
(talk about faith)

ikanbi pulled out his piece of black cloth
and untied it
so that a palm-nut and some earth fell into the river
plonk
plonk
then presto a palm-nut with sixteen fronds appeared
to the amazement of all

they scaled the tree and sat on the fronds
with the cock in tow
after resting awhile
they debated loud and long

what direction to take
until king okikisi the master of magic
appearing to the trumpeter
ordered him to blow again

he blew
and okanbi untied his black cloth
so that some earth fell into the river
and formed a small bank
which the cock espied
crowing with excitement
before flying down to scratch the earth with glee
and wherever earth met water
the water became land

the men hailed the new land with happy cries
but when they tried to climb down the tree
okanbi allowed only tetu and the trumpeter
for the rest had denounced him when in danger
and did not deserve to inhabit the new land
when they pled for pardon
okanbi let them stay on land with two conditions:
that they make him king
and pay two hundred cowries as tax each year

thus did okanbi become king of ife
where the land was fertile
and the food plentiful
the settlement soon grew into a town as others heard
came and steeled

okanbi married and had seven famous kids
the eldest was a girl
the mother of the first alaketu
the other children were sons
who became kings elsewhere in yorubaland
the youngest was oranyan
who built the empire of katunga
and okanbi lived to a ripe old age

spirit of imeren river

a woman lived with two young girls
molarin her daughter
and imeren her step-daughter
she saw molarin as a saint
and imeren as a scapegoat

one sunny afternoon mama went a-visiting
after asking the girls to wash a wooden water bowl
molarin broke the bowl by accident
and guess who got blamed by mama?

she beat imeren till she was black and blue
even as the girl insisted she was innocent
and while guilty molarin looked on
imeren wept her way out of the house

mama didn't bother to stop her
believing that hunger would soon bring her home
but imeren didn't return that day or the next

an alarmed mama sent a search part out into every home
bush nook and cranny
and still imeren could not be found

days later
molarin and mama went to get water from the river
with clay pots balanced gracefully on their heads
and talking all the while 'bout the missing girl

they put their pots down ready to get some water
when a loud voice sang

"who's calling imeren?
'twas molarin who broke the water bowl
yet you blamed imeren
who now lives in the middle of a forest deep in a swamp
where the sponge plant grows"

mother and daughter beat a hasty retreat
pots forgotten
they scuttled off to tell their neighbors about the mysterious voice

the neighbors went to the river
and found the tale was true
and hotfooted it from there too

when the king heard the strange tale
he led his chiefs to the river
but the voice sent them scurrying away

then the king sent for the wisest man in town
who had a huge head and a single leg
and when he limped to the palace
the king told him about the strange singing at the riverside
so the wise man went to see for himself

soon as he got there
the voice replayed its plaintive tune

"oh why d'you-all call imeren? why?
'twas molarin who broke the water bowl
yet you said imeren was to blame
now she lives in a forest far far away
down in the swamp where the sponge plant grows"

the wise man stood there in deep thought
then called aloud "imeren!
imeren! imeren! weep no more
we know the truth now
and will blame you no more
but never speak again
for you now live in the spirit world
but there may you sing and stay forever happy!"

with these words he switched off the voice
imeren never sang again
for her spirit was now at peace

today the river is named after her

problem child

kligbo's father was an efficient farmer
but kligbo himself was hyperactive and heedless

his parents tried their utmost to change him
and failed
so left him with these proverbial words:
a child who won't be taught at home
will be taught the hard way by strangers

one day kligbo told his dad he wanted his own farm
"thank God the boy's become serious" thought his father
so he advised kligbo to stay away from uncultivated land
devoid of palms and kolanut trees
for such land belonged to the evil spirits

when he left to find his own farm
kligbo came upon a piece of land
on which neither palms nor kolanut trees grew
anyone else would have left that land alone
but kligbo swore that spirit land or not
this would be his very own farm

so he went ahead and tilled the land
and as he worked
strange voices queried him
but the willful boy went on tilling

the voices vowed to help him
and before you could say "kligbo"
earth-spirits materialized
tilled the ground in no time
laughed eerily
and disappeared

kligbo flet he was a clever kid
and he began planting his seeds
when the voices questioned him again
he told them he was planting corn

the spirits re-emerged
did the planting then disappeared

our smart-alec rested awhile
dreaming of riches and fame
from harvesting and selling plenty of corn

he fell into a deep sleep
then woke
and when he saw the corn was almost ready to be reaped
his eyes popped like popcorn
and he stayed close to watch the corn

it ripened in the evening and he began to reap what he hadn't
                              sowed
again the voices intervened
to ask what he was doing

brimming over with confidence
he plucked the ears of corn
first the spirits assisted him
then destroyed the corn
and laughing coldly they left him

kligbo surveyed his devastated farm
and beat his head in remorse
when the spirits heard him
they helped him as they'd done before:
now
they beat him to death

a prince, a pauper and positive thinking

ages ago in the capital of the great oyo empire
lived the king called alaafin
his splendid palace gleamed with a hundred brass posts
and the princes were sent away to neighboring towns
to learn how to rule

one prince ruled the city of ikoyi
in a kindly and gentle fashion
not like the previous princes who were pompous and cruel

but the popular prince was miserable
for all the medicine men in the town couldn't help him and his wife
                              to have a child
elders of the town searched high and low in other towns
for a medicine man with the right magic
at long last one was found who prescribed some herbs
vowing that soon the prince and princess would have a son

the medicine man's pledge held fast
and soon the princess bore a son
everyone in ikoyi jumped from joy
as they showered the new baby with gifts galore
coweries and corn
yams and palm oil
chickens and goats
and innumerable names a la yoruba
the prince feted the new arrival in style
giving the people plenty to eat and drink

the child grew into a healthy and handsome lad
heir apparent to the popular prince
but just after he'd turned twelve
he died

weeping and wailing engulfed the town
and the woebegone prince planned to end his life
so to the forest he went to hang himself
as he made to put the noose around his neck
a voice cut thru his dark dreams
"hey wait a second
just who are you?"

the prince got jittery and dropped the rope
as an old bedraggled man emerged from nowhere
saying "fear not o son
it's only me
i live all alone

am almost blind
yet i see you're about to take your own life
why oh why do you wish to die?"

the prince told him of the passing of his only son

the old man told his own sad tale
how he used to be rich with a big house
many animals countless cowries
and a hundred relatives and servants living with him
until an epidemic raged thru the town
destroying everyone and everything
save him
alone
he cried himself almost blind
then went to live in the dense forest
"son you see i've suffered also
but i still have faith in the future
look at you a prince
you could yet become king
so go back home and await better days"

the prince was uplifted by the old man's words
and returned to town to find his father dead
the kingmakers in oyo had been searching for the prince
to make him king
so they gave him a grand welcome and he threw a party
gave the beggars many gifts

after his coronation the prince sent people to the forest
to fetch the old man which they did

the new king gave him a house
and servants to fulfill his every need
then called councillors
and told them of the old man's faith and how he foretold
                              a glorious future for the king
whose life he'd saved

the king made the old man the chief priest of the god of fate

the bashorun
years later the old man regained his sight
and lived happily in the palace till his death
after which the king and his councillors appointed a new bashorun
every time
as the most important chief in oyo

bashorun
the keeper of heavenly secrets
and worshipper of the god of fate

only the king
the queen mother
and the bashorun
know the secrets of the god of fate

the biggest orisha of all

at first there was _orisha_*
who lived alone in a small hut at the bottom of a big big rock
and owned a respectful but secretly rebellious slave

one day the slave lay in wait at the rock top
and as _orisha_ was returning from the farm
the slave rolled a bulky boulder onto the teeny-tiny hut

c-r-a-s-h!
orisha was crushed into countless pieces scattered worldwide

orunmila tried to save poor _orisha_
he travelled far and wide to pick up the pieces
then put the ones he could find into a huge calabash called
orisha nla
meaning
"the big _orisha_"
and placed it in a shrine in ife

but a myriad fragments of _orisha_ are still strewn all around
and so _orisha nla_ is considered the biggest _orisha_ of them all

*orisha - divinity

orisha oko

a farmer called orisha oko lived in irawo
and was famed for his knowledge of medicines and leaves

one year three huge black birds swooped on the fields and
                              devoured all the crops
famine followed and the same happened the next year
finally the farmers sought aid from orisha oko

he responded by brewing a potent medicine that drove the
                              destroyer birds away
so that the harvest was plentiful and the people rejoiced
and to show their gratitude they made orisha oko their king

soon they grew skeptical of his medical lore
perhaps recalling the yoruba proverb that says
"you are a king and you still want to make magic
do you want to become God?"
although he ruled justly their distrust intensified
one day they expelled him from the town

at harvest-time the next year
the big black birds returned
and devastated the fields once more

shamefaced they sought orisha oko's help again
promising to reinstate him and never again revolt
but orisha oko wouldn't oblige them now
for he couldn't put their faithlessness and inconstancy
                              out of his mind
his pain ran so deep
he vowed to forsake them forever
but he promised to leave his sword behind
so that if danger threatened their crops
they could drive his sword into the ground
and he would come to their aid

so saying
orisha oko vanished underground
today his sword is in the shrines where his worshippers go

ogun, god of iron and war

a fierce warrior was ogun
a mighty medicine man
whose charms were feared by all

one day his people drove him out of ire town
into a forest so dense and dark
he was trapped
and only on the seventh day
did he find a flintstone which he turned into a sharp sword
cut his way out of the forest
and returned to town

on arrival he fought with his followers
against the people who turned him out
and he became the warrior chief in town
famed for his fearsome sword

other warriors in other towns grew envious of his exploits and
fame
so with his enemies in ire
they plotted to bump him off

one day as ogun and family were working on the farm
a messenger came with news of an invasion by enemies from afar
causing panic to spread like a racy rumor
and a livid ogun swore to destroy the invaders with
                              his magic sword

while he was away fighting
some of his townsmen attacked his home
slew his son
while his wife and father managed to escape
before the traitors burned the house down

in a bid to blast ogun to bits

an epidemic soon seized the town
and people were dying in droves
so the few surviving elders consulted the ifa oracle
and found the gods were avenging
the death of ogun's son
the oracle further revealed
that until ogun and family came home
the epidemic would endure

the elders were contrite
the elders were quick
they sent emissaries into the forest to entreat ogun to return

it took some convincing but he consented to come home
on one condition only
he must have a dog and a tortoise first
the men would gladly have given him their right arms
so they provided the animals before you could say "ogun"

ogun, his family and the animals set out for the town
near the gates he ordered that the dog and the tortoise be killed
and that their blood be rubbed on his right big-toe
to check the epidemic

the messenger did as he was told
and when they entered ire
the epidemic ended
and the people sang and danced
months later
ogun went to the battleground in the sky
the people mourned his passing
gave him a befitting funeral
and deified him
they put his sword and weapons together in a palm-roofed hut
and sacrificed a dog to him
as a reminder of the time he put dog's blood on his tow
and arrested the epidemic

chichi layor

erinle and ogun

yemoja ogunle and her spouse ogun alagbede had three sons
eshu, akoro and igbo
eshu was naughty as they come and lived in elegba
akoro worked on the farm
and igbo was a hunter with dreadlocks
yemoja didn't let eshu into the house
for she couldn't cope with his trying ways

one day she consulted the oracle and was told
igbo wouldn't return if he went hunting during that moon
for osanyin the forest god was waiting to enchant him

yemoja hurried home to warn igbo against going out to hunt
but he disobeyed her as sons often do
meeting other hunters before a huge iroko tree
and each set out to hunt with a plan to return
to the same spot at the end of the hunt

igbo bumped into osanyin in the woods and the god befriended him
straightaway
then put him to sleep with a magic potion slipped into his drink
so that igbo selpt right thru the hunt
and woke to find he'd been turned into erinle
with no memory of his life as a human

the other hunters gathered beneath the iroko tree
blowing their horns to summon igbo
but they could have blown till the crows came home
the hunter with dreadlocks was gone for good

the others took the sad news home
and igbo's brother akoro resolved to find him
in their father's workshop he fabricated seven tools:
pickaxe-mattock-hatchet-scythe-lance-cutlass-shovel
he took the tools with him as he set out to seek igbo

he ventured deeper and deeper into the dense woods
clearing his way with the tools

when he saw igbo all feathered up and ready to go hunting
akoro hoisted him on his shoulders and carried him home

but yemoja wouldn't admit her disobedient son into her house
and swearing he couldn't bear to separate from igbo
akoro returned with him to the forest and became ogun

osanyin was heartbroken over his loss
so he went to seek igbo now known as erinle
and found him in the company of his brother ogun
now weary and worn out the three *orisha** agreed
to live in the forest together and share the same tools

yemoja was inconsolable over losing all three sons
so she hurled herself on the ground and became a river

her husband was the only one who died a natural death
so he didn't become an orisha with the power to take over
                              a human in a trance
and he has neither shrines nor worshippers

**orisha* - divinity

the impatient prince

when oduduwa reigned over ile-ife he sent his son ogun
                              on a warring spree
to overpower all surrounding towns and extend his empire

one day ogun lost his temper in ire-ekiti
demolishing everything and murdering the king
ogun beheaded him and put the gory object in a bag
then gathered the p-o-ws so he could march them to his father

news reached oduduwa's chiefs and they rushed to warn their king

that ogun wanted him dead so he could mount the throne
and he was on his way to present the onire's* head to oduduwa
an abomination for no king must ever see another king's
severed head

swift and decisive was oduduwa's response
a delegation was sent to meet ogun before he entered town
it took a display of diplimatic skills to get him to give them
the head

crisis over
ogun was taken to his father
in a desperate bid to please his bellicose son
oduduwa told him to take prisoners and booty and return
to ire-ekiti to rule

---

onire - the king of ire

ogun's chain

ogun the warrior couldn't sit still for a moment
strutting around like a bantam cock
always on the prowl looking for a fight
and bringing the booty back to father oduduwa in ife

he invaded ara and slew the alara*
ditto for ire and the onire*
then he installed his son as the new onire
and sauntered off to seek fresh conquests

twenty years later he sashayed back into town
bang in the middle of a special ceremony that forbade
participants to speak
ogun saw some gourds on the ground and floried in the thought
of quelling his thirst
and unaware that the gourds were empty
he asked the people for some palmwine
the people spoke not and that irked ogun who mistook

                          their ceremonial silence for discourtesy
drew his sword from its scabbard and slew a great number

when his rage abated and he saw his son the onire
he realized he'd killed his own people
and ravaged by remorse he resolved to leave the world
for every warrior must retire sometime

he told his people he would go under the ground
but he'd leave a length of chain above the ground
so that whenever they were attacked by their foes
they could pull the chain and ogun would reappear
having said that he vanished into the bowels of the earth

true to his word he resurfaced and defended the ire people
                          time and again
until a young doubter tested his elders' claims
he pulled the chain just to see what would ensue

ogun emerged and went on a rampage
killing right left and center
until the tide of his aggression ebbed
and he saw he had slain his compatriots

now ogun vowed never to return again

---

alara - the king of ara
onire - the king of ire

ogun and the foodseller

a poor foodseller consulted the ifa oracle
she sought to know how to make her business boom
she was told to sacrifice pigeons and chickens
and she promptly complied

days later ogun returned from a war
triumphant and rich to boot

his men's innards were agitated by hunger pangs
so he led them to the poor foodseller's stall
who served them all the food she'd cooked and more

when their hunger was sated they rose up to go
but ogun had no money to pay the foodseller for a job well done
so he bestowed an ample portion of his spoils on her
and the poor foodseller found herself suddenly rich   .

the first-ever egungun festival

long ago there lived a woman and her unruly child
ojulari
spoilt silly by his mother
for he was her only living child

one day he covered face and body with her cloth
and danced all day long
happy as a lark
while his mother looked on with a lazy smile
then sang and drummed in accompaniment
till the boy danced himself to sleep

next day he tried to play back the scene
but his mother was too busy to beat her makeshift drum today
he threw a terrible tantrum now
as some kids are wont to do when they don't get their way
ojulari's mom waited for his mood to pass
hoping he'd soon go out to play

he didn't
and his sulking did not cease
when he fell ill with fever the following day
his mom panicked
remembering her other children had died from fever

she went to consult the ifa oracle
and was advised to meet ojulari's every demand

like lightning she flew home
and dressed her son in a sack
then beat her wooden stool like a drum as she'd done before

the sick boy rose and began to dance
till the fever left him and lo he was well

from then on he always asked her to drum on her stool
while he danced
and she dared not refuse for the oracle had warned
she must meet the boy's every demand
or he'd fall sick again

thus it was that she had no time to work
while ojulari became a right pain in the neck
demanding drumming and food in an endless cycle
eko* and moyinmoyin*
ra-pa-pam-pam
eko and moyinmoyin
and whips to keep the goats from eating his food

the poor woman was highly stressed by all this
her whole life revolved around her son's requests
so that aging rapidly
she breathed her last

by then ojulari was a man
and was filled with remorse for wearing out his devoted mom
so he vowed to keep her memory alive

he had friends come over
served them eko and moyinmoyin like his mother used to feed him
then gave them sacks to cover themselves
and they danced with him down the streets
carrying whips reminiscent of the ones his mother used to keep
                              the goats away
while a drummer drummed without skill like his mother used to do

his descendants carried on the family tradition
every year

and ojulari is now called the father of egunguns

yorubas believe
the spirits of their ancestors return to earth
as egunguns
the egungun of ibadan blessed the olubadan* and all
the inhabitants
then prays for peace
a rich harvest
and good fortune

the egunguns cover themselves completely
when they dance in the streets
displaying their magic and masked faces
and speaking thru their noses like people with bad colds

and now a song from the egungun repertoire

"i come softly as the showers at night
i come easily as the dew at dawn
i come quickly as the showers at sunrise
i come to stop farmers from going to the farm
i come to stop her that goes to the stream at dawn
i come to stop children from crying for the breast
behold i come into the world with an only child"

---

* _eko_ - steamed corn flour
* _moyinmoyin_ - steamed bean flour
* _olubadan_ - the king of ibadan, a town in yorubaland

the origin of tribal marks

king shango planned to conquer oyo
but first he wished to find out his late mother's name
for she died when he was just a child

now he knew she was the daughter of the king of the tapa
so he sent two slaves to tapaland

to sacrifice to his mother in the king's court
and to listen for her name during the royal ritual

one of the slaves was a hausaman whose attention often strayed
but the other slave listened carefully and found out
torosi

shango chastised the hausa slave by ordering him to receive
a hundred and twenty-two cuts
but the resulting scars seemed to please the king's wives
so to humor them shango had two long marks carved
on his own arm
fearsome strokes running from shoulder to thumb
the *eyo* mark is reserved for the royal family
even now

next shango sent the hausa slave to the oloyokoro
the king of oyo
with this message:
"i myself have lovely marks like these
i know you and your chiefs would like them too"

three days later
the oloyokoro and his chiefs lay in pain
in their newly scarified skin
recuperating from their drastic surgery

shango then invaded the city
with ease

the first circumcision

olorun created egun and a woman called olure
then he told them both to go into the world
but olure wished to go alone
so ogun stayed in the sky

as olure was capering along in carefree joy
she came upon a mighty tree that lay across the road

and realizing she needed a brawny he-man
she went back to olorun and begged
"please oh please send ogun to cut up the tree"

ogun came and while he worked
olure watched with legs apart in unladylike fashion
suddenly a chip of wood sailed straight between her legs
and when ogun was through he returned to his dwelling in the sky

the wood chip caused olure considerable pain
so back she went to olorun to ask
would he please send ogun to take the chip out?

ogun would do so only if she agreed to marry him
in her agony she forgot to act coy but consented
at once
after he extracted the chip with his knife
a conspicuous scar remained and that's how female
                                        circumcision began

she went first and he followed behind
and to this day women walk ahead of their husbands
showing utter disrespect for men

ogun and olure then went to ado-ekiti where they made love
and to speed up the sperm flow
he cut off the tip of his penis and that's how male
                                        circumcision began

the oro cult

pakunde close-the-door consulted the oracle for asehim
                                    bokin of iseyin*

the asehin's problem problem was this
his wives were all barren
so how prove his virility?
ifa oracle said to offer a sacrifice to his father
the asehin complied but his father spurned him

100

he went to see his mother who then said
his natural father wasn't human at all
and then she told the strangest tale

one day she went to get firewood from the farm
when a gorilla raped her
she revenged by using a clever ruse
splitting a tree with her axe she asked the gorilla to put
                                his penis in the crack
the horny creature did so and she pulled out the axe
so that his penis was trapped and he died
and that was the reason the asehin's ostensible father
not being his natural father
rejected the asehin's sacrifice
people knew the *oro* or gorilla died in a tree

the asehin made for the forest right there and then
he found the gorilla's bones
and slaughtered a ram
then had the carcass carried into the town
singing all the while

"close the doors for *oro* is coming
the son is carrying his father
landlords close your doors
the son is carrying his father home
oro is coming"

they dangled the body in the air
and people said
truly this is a dead person speaking
and still they call it *oro* today

---

iseyin - a town 27 miles from oyo in yorubaland

osanyin

ifa came into the world
and he wanted a slave to work on his farm

101

chichi layor

so he bought one from the market
and told him to cut the grass in the fields

the slave saw that the grass he was about to cut
was the grass that cures fever
so he restrained his arm

he tried to cut another kind of grass
but saw it was the grass for headaches

he tried to cut yet another kind
but saw it was the grass for stomachaches

so the learned slave left the medicinal grasses untouched

news reached ifa who sent for his slave
the renowned herbalist osanyin
and in order to learn the lore of herbs
ifa made osanyin always stay by his side

king oranmiyan

in the beginning the earth did not exist
only the sky above and the water below
both devoid of any form of life
olodumare first created seven crown princes
and seven calabashes of corn gruel for food
also seven bags of cowries, beads and cloth
twenty iron bars
one chicken
an unknown object tied up in black cloth
and a lengthy chain
to which he hitched the princes' food and other stuff
before letting it down into the world

next olodumare flung a palm-nut down from the sky
and instantly a mighty palm tree appeared
the princes settled down on its branches with the treasures
                            provided by olodumare

they were called olowu, onisabe, orangun, oni, ajero, alaketu,
and oranmiyan
and they became the kings of egba, sabe, ila, ife, ijero, ketu,
and oyo respectively

all seven princes were power-crazy and couldn't stay together
each captain would command his own ship
so they separated and divided up the treasures thus:

six princes kept cowries, beads, cloth, food
leaving the youngest the mysterious cloth and the iron bars
then the six older princes melted into the branches of the palm tree

leaving their kid brother high and dry

poor oranmiyan untied the black cloth
and found a strange black substance inside
which he threw into the water thinking it was trash

the black substance became a mound of earth
onto which the chicken flew down
and scratched furiously so that the earth spread all over the water

and a vast land was formed

an overjoyed oranmiyan took over the new land
still holding on to his twenty iron bars
but his six brothers saw him from their palm tree and climbed
down to claim the land as they'd claimed the other treasures

this time their ignoble quest was fated to fail
for the iron bars changed into weapons of many kinds:
arrows, machets, spears, and swords

oranmiyan seized a gleaming sword with a razor-sharp blade
and set upon the six greedy princes with these words:

"this here is my earth and mine alone
up on that tree you all robbed me of my rightful share
leaving me only the earth and the iron

now this land and these arms
unworthy brothers
i swear i'll slay you all"

the greedy six promptly prostrated before him
pleading for pardon
and he forgave them on one condition
they and their progeny would be ruled by him and his own
                                          children
and every year they would come to the capital city and
                                   pay homage to him

thus did oranmiyan come to be king of the yorubas and
                                  of all the world

how oranmiyan founded oyo

oranmiyan succeeded oduduwa as king of ife
one day the people prepared to sacrifice a lady slave to obatala
but finding she was pregnant they let her live
and dedicated the child in her womb to obatala
the creator god

the child became obatala's priest
and the older he grew the more responsibilities he was given
in the end the king put all shrines under his care

when oranmiyan wished to go to war with the nupe people
he rallied his chiefs and his army and marched on the river niger
leaving obatala's priest to look after ife

at the river oranmiyan found the nupe army ready and waiting
                                  on the other side
with bows and arrows they blocked the advance
                                  of oranmiyan's army

shamefaced
he consulted with his chiefs
and resolved there and then to found a new town

so he asked his friend the king of borgu
to tell him where to settle down
the king of borgu put a charm round a boa constrictor's neck
and said the snake would lead oranmiyan to a new town

the snake slithered along to a certain spot where it
                                        went underground

and there oranmiyan founded oyo
but when he wished to be crowned alafin
he had to get permission from the priest in ife
to use some ritual things for his coronation

then owuoni the son of the slave became ruler of ife
now known as the oni
and no alafin of oyo is ever installed
unless he receives ritual objects from the oni of ife

oranmiyan's mother

kind oduduwa of ife was an albino
but ogun his son was charcoal-black

one day the king sent ogun to the ogotun war
there he fought fearlessly and over-powered his foes
handing all other prisoners to his father
ogun kept the comely maiden lakange and swiftly wedded her

news of the nuptials angered the king
who sent his servants to wrest her from his son
then he married her knowing full well she'd been deflowered
                                        by ogun

she bore a bizarre bi-colored child
white on the right
black on the left
ogun named the freak baby oranmiyan
meaning
"my word has triumphed"

105

oranmiyan grew up and went to benin as king
when oduduwa died in ife his first son obalufon succeeded him
and following the tradition he inherited his father's wives
including the graceful lakange
beloved mother of oranmiyan

the news reached him thru the grapevine
and leaving his son eweka to rule benin in his stead
oranmiyan made a mad dash to ife
after sending advance death threats to half-brother obalufon
who fled to iddo oshun and later to ifon
oranmiyan arrived in ife and took his mother back
then cowned himself king of ife

his tomb in ife can still be seen today

heads of fate

mokewure the priest of goats
and mojewara the priest of sheep
consulted the ifa oracle for three children:
orisanku the son of ogun
oritemere the son of ija
and afuwape the son of orunmila

these children wished to come into the world
but each must choose his own fate
none of them knew what to do or how to choose
only orunmila consulted the oracle for his son
and was told afuwape would be a successful man
but first orunmila had to offer a sacrifice

in compliance with the oracle's instructions
he gave his son a thousand cowries to be spent in the house
                                        of ajalamo
the one who moulds new children

orisanku and oritemere waited awhile for afuwape
but he didn't show up and they had to leave

for ajalamo's house

they found no one there
but they saw several beautiful heads of fate
they hadn't a clue which to choose
finally they picked what they felt were the most promising heads
and then sallied forth into the world

much later afuwape came to ajalamo's house
but he saw only an old woman sitting on the floor
she said she was waiting for ajalamo to come pay for the
                                        corn beer he'd bought
when afuwape asked how much she was owed
she said it was a thousand cowries
so he gave her the money his dad had given him

she thanked him and asked what he'd come to do
he said it was to choose his own head
she told him two boys had come earlier and picked their
                                        own heads
then she hobbled away

immediately
ajalamo jumped down from the rafters where
he'd been hiding all along
he thanked afuwape most profusely for paying his debt
then led the child to the garden where
all the heads were arrayed
so many becutiful heads afuwape saw
but ajalamo told him

"beware of those beautiful heads
they aren't the best heads
some who choose them don't succeed in the world
others who pick them are plagued by enemies
people bring sorrow on themselves by picking the wrong heads
my friend
here is the right head for you
my boy
i give you my blessing as you go into the world

107

afuwape became a wealthy man
surprising orisanku and oritemere who began to sing

"didn't he pick his head from the same place as we
everyone's fate is different
so different
if i knew where afuwape got his own head
boy i'd go get mine again"

the rock and the river

oba oke of otan had a lovely daughter whom he loved very much
never mind that she had four breasts
a secret known only to her parents and her

when otin grew up her father urged her to remain a bachelor girl
for much as a husband might love her
he would reveal her secret flaw in a fit of rage one day
so although she felt lonely she heeded her father's words

she lived alone for years in a neighboring town
there she was a trader in the local market
one fine day a hunter came to the market and was so
                                        captivated by her looks
that he promptly proposed to marry her

her refusal finally wore thin
and the dogged hunter accepted her strict condition
no he would never breathe a word to anyone about her four breasts
and he gave his own stipulation:
she must never put ewedu* leaf in his soup
for his orisha forbade him to eat that leaf

they were happy together
she was his favorite wife
until the other wives hatched a heinous plan
one the day it was otin's turn to cook for their husband
the envious wives slipped ewedu into his soup

when poor otin was in the bathroom

the hunter returned and sat down to eat the food cooked by
                                        his favorite wife
right away he tasted the taboo leaf
his wrath was boundless as he battered poor otin
calling her a four-breasted daughter of a cow

the word went round
the invective echoed everywhere
and a distressed otin sought refuge in her father's arms
he consoled her as best he could
but she feared the jeering would follow her to her father's arms

in the depths of her despondency she strayed into the woods
and casting herself on the ground she became a raging river
her troubled father had been tailing her and what he saw
                                        made him despair
so he turned himself into a steadfast stone
and today
oke rock and otin river are worshipped in otan

---

* ewedu - an edible leaf

yemanja

ravishing yemanja had a secret flaw
she had only one breast
and fearful that a husband might disclose her secret
she refrained from getting married

walking home from the market one day
the disabled lady bewailed her fate
"oh to be so lonesome without a man
on one to cook and care for
no one to squabble with
and a home without children
oh woe is me"

creeping up behind her
ogun overheard
and in a fit of passion he proposed to her
"yemanja do not fear my fierce mien
deep down i'm really a softie you'll see
marry me and i'll take good care of you
and defend you against an unfriendly world
only promise you'll never mention my bloodshot eyes"

she accepted his proposal with her own proviso:
he must never touch her single breast
they married and both kept their vows
many children followed and all went well for a time

then one day ogun wishing to rejoice his woman's heart
went into the kitchen to cook for her
but he wasn't good at women's work and so be bungled it
dropping the pot and spilling the soup all over the place

the noise work yemanja from her beauty sleep
and she ran to the kitchen to investigate
when she saw ogun standing there and looking like a periwinkle
                                        out of its shell
she blew her top and bawled him out

"waddya think you're doing you and your bloodshot eyes?!"

her rash words made ogun apoplectic with rage
and he knocked her down to the ground
then wracked by remorse he tried to soothe her
going down on his knees
he caressed her breast

this made yemanja tremble and then
she melted into water and slipped thru his fingers
ogun was crushed by the loss of his wife
so swearing that tenderness did not suit him
he stormed out of his home and resumed his martial lifestyle

110

sakpata the god of suffering

molusi the hunter saw an antelope in the woods
but when he tried to shoot
it put up a front paw and darkness descended at midday

when daylight returned
molusi saw aroni
a forest spirit with one leg

aroni promised the hunter a potent charm
and told him what he must do
you know
rituals and things
then it gave him a leaf to plant near his home
and a whistle with which to call aroni to his aid

seven days later
smallpox struck the city residents
claiming a myriad lives
so the hunter returned to the forest
and at the sound of his whistle the spirit appeared
and was told the charm it produced was a deadly one

it said the gift was sakpata
not a charm
and the hunter could prevent further deaths by building
                              a shrine for sakpata
who must be obeyed by all
the spirit told of rituals to be performed
and it provided the needed leaves
explaining how sakpata could kill then resuscitate his followers

aroni then gave the hunter a charm to heal the already sick
they say this all happened at vedji near dassa zoume
                              in the republic of benin

111

shonponna the king who hurts the world

the-dog-is-selling-honey-in-the-market
and
the-dog-is-looking-at-me
were two babalawos* who consulted the ifa oracle
or ogun eshu orisha-oko shango orunmila dn shonponna

there once lived a man called babaniyangi
a father of five:
ogun, eshu, orisha-oko, shango, orunmila, and shonponna

from his deathbed in heaven the man sent for his children
but they arrived too late
he had already passed on
so they performed the funeral rites for seven days
then began their journey back to the world

en route they grew thirsty and stopped to rest beneath
                                     an iroko tree
they sent shonponna to get water from the river which was
                                     a longways off

when he left
they shared papa's property among themselves
his horse his clothes his money and much more

shonponna returned to see he'd been tricked
and he stormed off in a frenzy
orunmila called him back to say if he went to heaven
he could pick up his own share there
a bow and an arrow
a stick and a string

shonponna went to heaven and found the things
and on his way back he bumped into orunmila
whom he asked to consult the oracle for him
but orunmila sent his apprentice instead

the apprentice awolaje consulted the oracle

112

and was told that shonponna would outstrip his brothers
if only he would offer sacrifices
shonponna did as he was directed
going to his father's grave to change the incantations
his father spoke to him saying he would surpass his brothers
and that his share of the inheritance was not without value

a heartened shonponna returned to the world
and chanting incantations he shot his arrows to the
                              four corners of the earth
swiftly unleashing smallpox on his birthplace in nupeland

the people sought to know from orunmila the source of this
                              strange sickness
he told how they cheated shonponna out of his rightful share
                              of his father's bequest
and he told the people to sacrifice to shonponna and thereby
                              plead his pardon

so the king and all the people worshipped shonponna
and the disease was divested of its deadly power
henceforth shonponna was renamed obaluaiye
meaning
"the king who hurts the world"

orunmila and his runaway wife

orunmila and iwa had been married for many years
but they were yet to hear the patter of tiny feet
so a depressed iwa went to the oracle
the priest told her to marry the ajero of ijero
and she would then be blessed with a child

her bio-clock was fast ticking away
so she hurried to ijero and hung around the palace
the king espied her and his heart flipped
then he married her and her dream came true
at long long last she had a child

orunmila found her and tried to win her back
but iwa escaped to ara and married the alara
the king of ara
again she produced another prince
and still orunmila pursued her

iwa fled to ila and married the orangun of ila
and as they were starting to enjoy connubial bliss
along came orunmila to queer their pitch

he maintained that he hadn't come to claim his ex-wife
all he wanted was a small room
where he'd live and be near his broody love

the orangun granted his request
perhaps out of pity for the infertile man
iwa had many children for the orangun
while orunmila lived quietly in the palace
not bothering anyone

how orunmila became an orisha

one day orunmila disappeared down the elephant's anus
orunmila's followers were frantic and they sent for the
                                    experts in elephant anatomy
ogun and oshosi cut up the elephant skillfully
but behold orunmila wasn't in there
only a wooden tray and a calabash containing sixteen
                                    pairs of palm-nits

they gave sixteen nuts to the alara
and sixteen to the ajero and both became kings
they say orunmila went to heaven to live forever more

orunmila the powerful

orunmila was needling his followers:
he asked "don't you see that awful thing coming down the road?"

they answered "no"
"anyone seen my brother lasope?"
"yeah, we've met him"
"how's he doing?"
"okay -- he's got six wives and they're all okay"
"so you met lasope and his six wives and they're all okay huh?
then what about me?"
"you? you're like an iroko tree in the forest
a mighty immovable tree"
"how dare you compare me to a mere tree?"
"orunmila we know you're very clever but
will you please please please leave us alone?"
"where shall i go?"
"to the house of iki the palm tree"
"i already went there and he made me welcome"
"well then go see imo the palm leaf"
"i did that already -- he's my good friend you know"
"have you gone to ootu ife where your worshippers are?"
"yeah way back when you were this small"
"when was that again?"
"when the whip was called kusonoro and the cudgel iyapo"
"hah that's a very -- well -- ordinary story
surely the great orunmila can do better than that"

orunmila lost his cool and bellowed
"look at my right hand
you two hundred people fall down and die!"

they fell down as if he'd switched their lives off

so the survivors quickly said
"we'll worship you mesiakaraba
we'll worship you onikehin ahagun esinrani"
"how will you worship me?"
"with our head like the rat in the bush
with our head like the fish in the stream"

orunmila then ordered
"you igigbegi will be the priest in the forest
you ootipa will be the priest in the palm tree plantation

115

look at my right hand
you two hundred people wake up!
look at my left hand
you two hundred people wake up!
the electric fish has come
ifa it is you who wake up the dead!"

from that day on orunmila's devotees have never doubted him
always they follow him faithfully

obatala and oduduwa

ooldumare sent obatala and oduduwa to create the world
using the bag of the world they carried along

en route they rested and drank some palmwine
obatala sank into a drunken stupor
and oduduwa had to go on alone
until he arrived on earth and found water everywhere

opening the bag of the world he brought out some dirt
and built a little island on the water
then he took a five-toed cock
and put it down on the ground
the cock scratched the earth
here there and everywhere
in true chicken style

in this way did oduduwa create the world
soon sixteen major orisha came down from heaven
and lived with im in ile-ife

the calabash of good character

olodumare gave oduduwa and obatala a magic calabash
wished them luck as they journeyed into the world

on the way they saw a women laden with palmwine

obatala drank his senses away
leaving oduduwa to carry the calabash of good character
                              back to olodumare
who then allowed him to use the calabash

when obatala became sober he ran to oduduwa in a rage
demanding to know why the calabash had disappeared

the kindly olodumare showed him how to create people
                              and animals
the greatest art of all

from then on obatala vowed to abstain from palmwine
for he was now he who creates the son and the mother
the nose and the eyes

why obatala loves the disabled

obatala created man from clay
he moulded men and women
and olodumare breathed life into them

on the day obatala drank too much palmwine
he made hunchbacks, albinos, the blind, the deaf, the dumb
                              and the lame

thereafter all disabled people became sacred to him
and dwelled in his shrine

now obatala and his devotees abstain from palmwine

shango's mother

shango's mother obatala* was weighed down with work
she wasn't superwoman so she sought ifa's advice
the oracle told her to go to her son's home
but first she must offer corn as a sacrifice
ifa warned that three mishaps would befall her on the way

117

and yet she must be silent and struggle on

first she met eshu masked as a seller of charcoal
who wanted help with lifting the load onto his head
obatala obliged and to show his gratitude
eshu ran coal-black hands over her white dress
not a squeak escaped obatala's lips
in compliance with ifa's command

farther down the road she saw a fruit-seller
it was eshu disguised anew
he asked her to lift a basket from his head
obatala obliged and to show his gratitude
eshu stained her dress with fruit
not a squeak escaped obatala's lips
in compliance with ifa's command

she continued her journey with some corn cobs under her arm
until she came to a forest stricken with drought
in which shango's long-lost horse had been hiding for twelve years

the hungry horse followed her with an intent to steal
she chased it away but it always returned
woman and horse acted out a slapstick comedy
until they were sighted by shango's soldiers
who recognized the runaway horse
and hauled the hapless woman before shango's throne

he received his mother with uncontrollable joy
many years had elapsed since they last met
shango then erected a house for her
and blended his red beads with her own white ones
now shango's devotees wear the _kele_ necklace with red
                              and white beads
while obatala's devotees wear plain white beads called _sesefun_

---

* Editor's note: Although Obatala is a male god, creator of human
beings, this tale about a mother named Obatala suggests its early
origins, when gods were frequently androgynous. One early story
says that the slave Atunda rolled a boulder onto Obatala, who broke
into myriad pieces, all of which became gods.

shango's friend

old obatala hadn't seen king shango for a real long time
so he decided to go a-visiting
but first he went to see a *babalawo** to find out if he should go

the priest consulted the ifa oracle and came up with this:
should obatala go on that trip he would die
but the old man yearned to see his friend and he asked if
                                sacrifices couldn't fend off his fate

the priest was loath to intercede but he was sensitive to
                                obatala's pleas
and finally the father of secrets conceded this:
great suffering would dog obatala's steps
but the trip could be taken without ending in death
provided these rules were followed:

never complain or take revenge or refuse to do a kind of service
and do take along three white robes, black soap, and shea butter
and yet great suffering will follow you every step of the way

obatala started out slowly using his walking stick
and after plodding awhile he stumbled upon eshu sitting
                                by the road
with a big pot of palm oil by his side
eshu told the old man to help him put the pot on his head
obatala obliged and in return eshu poured the oil
                                over the old man's head

he recalled the rules he'd been given and so didn't complain
rather he went down to the river where he washed himself
spread shea butter all over his age-racked body
donned a clean white robe
and took to the road once more

twice more eshu played a cruel trick on obatala
over whom he poured charcoal dust
and plenty of red palm oil
both times the old man refrained from reacting to eshu's jeering

119

and both times he bathed in the river and changed his robe

at last he arrived in shango's kingdom of oyo
and recognized a royal horse on the run
then trapped it and as he was feeding it with corn
along came shango's servants and charged him with horse theft
hauled him into town and straight into jail

then followed seven disastrous years in oyo -
drought
epidemics
barren women
what could be worse?

finally shango consulted the ifa oracle and found
the calamity was caused by the unjust imprisonment of one man
shango probed the issue and when obatala was brought before him
the king recognized his old friend

sounds of merry reunion rent the air
and shango ordered his servants to wash obatala in complete
                              silence as a show of respect
then he dressed his friend in rich white robes
and sent him home laden with luxurious gifts

---

* _babalawo_ - literally, father of secrets, priest of ifa oracle

obatala and the witches

obatala worked at creating men from clay
every day he needed water to mix the clay
so each morning before anyone else was up
he went down to the river to draw some water

then came a drought and all the rivers dried up
not a drop of water could be found anywhere
so the witches dug a well in the woods for their own use

obatala found out about the witches' well
and helped himself to the water as often as he liked
but he failed to sacrifice as the *babalawos** advised
and soon the witches decided to stop the thief
so they sprang a trap that snared him on the fifth day
in spite of his pleas they refused to pardon him
but he slipped away to egungun's home
and egungun pledged to protect him

the witches appeared outside the house
and asked egungun to hand over the thief
he refused but when they threatened to destroy his powers
he hurriedly handed over obatala

this time he escaped to the home of shango
the god of thunder
who promised to placate the witches

they came swiftly to shango's door demanding that he return
                                    the refugee
and ignoring shango's passionate pleas
they vowed to destroy his staff and thunderbolt
so poor shango let them take obatala

now he hurried to orunmila's home
where the priest awoyeroye was consulting the oracle
the priest told orunmila a stranger would appear
and told the god to offer a sacrifice
*ekuru**
glue
and four hundred cowries
later the priest said to put glue round the edges of a tray
                                    full of *ekuru*

orunmila obeyed
and soon obatala came running in
begging to be protected from the persistent witches
but orunmila assured him everything would be all right

along came the witches in quick pursuit

seeking to recapture the runaway thief
orunmila invited the witches to a meal
but they insisted they hadn't come to eat
so orunmila chanted the *odu** that awoyeroye taught him
and the witches suddenly agreed to eat
they sat around the tray to eat the bean cakes
and while they ate
the glue held their feathers firm
they got up to go and found they couldn't move
so they begged orunmila to set them free
promising to spare obatala and his progeny
in return for their release

they were freed and they kept their word
later obatala rewarded orunmila with a special gift:
an iron bell or *ajila*
to be rung whenever orunmila went out at night

today during nocturnal outings
all ifa priests ring an iron bell
to clear evil from their path
and orunmila would sing:

"it belonged to orisha*
this iron in my hand
it belonged to orisha"

---

* *babalawo* - priest of ifa oracle
* *ekuru* - bean cakes
* *odu* - section or chapter of a body of recitals on divination
        connected with the cult of orunmila

obatala and the blind fisherman

obatala-the-powerful can make a blind man see

two *babalawos** consulted the oracle for a blind fisherman
called ojiya ego
whose fish was always being stolen

122

because he couldn't see

ifa told the blind man what to sacrifice
and taught him to sing this song at the riverside:

"i know who stole my fish
lenle lenle nlere o lenle lenle
he wears a white gown
lenle lenle nlere of lenle lenle
and white metal on his writs
lenle lenle nlere o lenle lenle
i know who stole my fish"

obatala heard the song and was stunned
for the blind man's description suited him to a tee
he'd been using the fish to prepare a charm that gave him
                                        supreme power
now he implored ojiya to keep the theft a secret
or the god's reputation would be ruined for sure

ojiya saw his chance and seized it at once
he wanted the god to restore his sight in return
obatala complied and from that day on
his followers were forbidden to eat fish

---

* *babalawo* - priest of ifa oracle

shango the pretender

one day shango changed into a little laddie
and off he went to topple the king
when the king asked whose child shango was
on one admitted to knowing him
so the king ordered him to be killed and thrown in the river

the king's men obeyed but when they came back
the boy was again before the throne
the king was baffled by this bizarre affair

and he decided women would do the killing this time

the women followed in hot pursuit
but shango eluded them with tricks and taunts
he jumped over a huge hole and scaled a tall tree
then dashed to the woods and climbed another tree
from there he hanged himself with a rope
till he was a dead as a dry leaf

the women went to the king to report his death
and the king ordered a special sacrifice
a cow, a ram, a cock, a wild duck, a guinea fowl, a chicken,
        a pidgeon, a snail, a tortoise, some oil and shea butter
the servants were instructed to dig a ditch under shango's
        hanging body
they threw in the sacrifice and severed the rope

the corpse fell off the tree and lo the boy was alive again
people couldn't believe their eyes and ears
for shango squealed "i didn't hang myself"

the king went to the woods to see for himself the immortal child
and when he returned
shango had taken his place
the king ordered him to descend
but the brazen boy wouldn't budge
claiming he was the oba koso
meaning
the new king

shango meets his match

shango was oranmilan's son and a warrior king
a terror to the neighbors and a plague to his people
who were war-weary and begged the king to stop his
                        frequent raids
for their sons were being slain in battle
and who would plant their crops?
shango would have given in to his people's pleas

but his army leaders wouldn't hear of it
for they raked in riches from the many raids

the army chiefs posed a special challenge
they were timi and gbonka the hotheads
shango decided to set them against each other
thereby hoping to smother both flames
timi was in charge of ede
a boundary town
but he'd become full of himself
and now acted like a king

shango sent gbonka to fight timi
but timi faced him with his deadly arrows
gbonka himself was armed with powerful charms
and put a spell on timi to make him sleep
before bearing him off to oyo town

shango was scared of gbonka and ordered a rerun
and a new venue for the duel:
the akesan market in oyo
again gbonka put his opponent to sleep
then sealed his victory by beheading timi

a power-drunk gbonka now dared the king:

"kabiyesi you thought i'd be killed didn't you?
people fear you because of the fire that comes out of your mouth
but kabiyesi your so-called fire can't tough me

"light a large fire oh people of oyo
pour shea butter and oil on the flames
then tie me up with the toughest rope
and throw me in the fire but it won't touch me!"

they threw him in the fire expecting him to be barbecued
but not a hair of his head was harmed
he warned shango to resign or risk being driven off the throne

the terrified people all deserted their king

leaving only his senior wife oya
together the two sought refuge in his mother's hometown
                              tapa in nupeland
there in humiliation he hanged himself
and they say he climbed into the sky on a chain

his loyal wife assembled his pals and they paraded the town
singing as they did so
"oba koso"
meaning
"the king did not hang himself"
soon they succeeded in restoring his authority in oyo
and shango protected his supporters with lightning and thunder

shango and the magic tree

shango
the youngest son of oranmiyan and yamase
was no warrior and so his brothers detested him

but he was his father's favorite son
and when oranmiyan prepared to pass on
he stored his wealth in a hollow tree in the woods
and told shango

"soon as i join my ancestors
go hang yourself from that tree in the woods
i already showed it to you
and if you're ever in a jam
go see the magician onikoso"

when oranmiyan died shango's brothers molested him
but remembering his father's words
he went to the forest to hang himself
the hollow tree collapsed and oranmiyan's wealth tumbled out

shango garnered the riches and ran
to a virgin area where he set up roots
living in peace with his neighbors and not waging any wars

so that people were drawn from other places
by the peace and endless feasts

news reached his brothers at whose hearts envy gnawed
and they prepared to take over shango's new land
he quivered at the thought of war and quickly sought
                              the magician's help

oniloso prepared a potent charm for shago to place in his mouth
but shango couldn't collect it himself and sent his wife oya
curiosity clawed at her and she ate some of the charm
                              from the calabash
thus disobeying onikoso's orders

instantly
flames flowed out of her mouth
for she was now an *orisha**
she went to shango's palace and he ate the charm too
his mouth spewed fire which devoured his foes
his brothers ate the charm and became *orisha* as well

shango's people took fright at his fiery mouth
and sent him parrots' eggs as a sign of rejection
a melancholy shango made for the forest once more
seeking to hang himself again
soon as he put the noose around his neck
the ground gave way beneath his feet and he vanished
                              underground

his faithful servant raced back to town to report the strange affair
and they came to survey the chasm down which shango had sunk
but while they mourned his mysterious passing
he sent huge stones up into the air
killing all who said he was dead

---

* *orisha* - a divinity

thunder chases wind

shango's medicine made him spit fire from his mouth
men and orisha* were terrified
shango asked his wife to keep some medicine for him
but she swallowed it instead
so he went after her with murder in his heart
and she fled to olokun her brother and god of the sea

shango chased her and fought with olokun over her
but she ran to her sister olosa the lagoon
still shango followed fast
and when olosa saw him she begged him on bended knee
to forgive her sister

now shango had a weakness for pretty women
so he and olosa made love
leaving oya free to flee to lokoro near porto novo

in the end shango forgave her but her fear remained
and when shango trails an enemy oya always flees
now you see why oya's wind goes before shango's thunder

---

* _orisha_ - divinities

shango and huisi

his potent medicine made shango the most feared king
                              in yorubaland
some of the medicine was carried in his mouth
and his words were followed by famished flames
he put the rest of the medicine in his wife oya's care
but jealous oya concealed the magic calabash

shango was enraged by her brazen act
and he rushed after her but she fled to her brother olokun
he followed her to the spot where sky and water meet
and there he struggled with olokun over her

128

oya then ran to her sister olosa the lagoon
again shango chased her and she retreated to the home of a man
                                     called huisi
who told her no human could fight an *orisha** like shango
but she gave him some of shango's medicine to eat
and huisi himself became an *orisha*
he tore a mighty tree from its roots and attacked shango

shango gave as good as he got and the fight was a draw
and as an incensed shango stamped his foot
the ground yawned and swallowed him and huisi
oya escaped to lokoro near porto novo
where a shrine was built to honor her

---

* *orisha* - a divinity

oya's gift

oya was part-antelope and part-woman
every five days she went to market as a woman
after hiding her antelope-skin in the woods

one day in the market shango met a lady of elegance
and followed her to find out where she lived
he watched her go into the woods and wear her skin
and become a full-fledged antelope again

next market day shango hid in the woods
waiting for oya to turn into a woman
when she left for the market shango moved fast
picked up her skin and took it home

he returned to the woods and found a forlorn oya seeking her skin

he consoled then married her
he had two other wives oshun and oba
but they'd borne him no children

and soon oya was the proud mother of twins
an event that put the other wives right in the shade

jealous and suspicious
they hounded their husband with queries:
who was this strange woman
what was her family
and how did he meet her?

the more persistent wife finally wore shango down
and he confided in her the secret of oya's origins
and how her antelope-skin lay under the roof
he swore the jealous wife to secrecy
but she soon was singing a sly song:

"oh she eats and she drinks
but her skin lies under the roof"

oya heard and her excitement knew no bounds
as soon as she was alone she looked under the roof and found
                                        her precious skin
donned it and skipped back into the woods
as merry an antelope as you ever saw

when shango got home he raced after her and sought to woo her
                                        once more
but she charged at him with her wicked horns
he calmed her by giving her a plate of savory *akara**
that was her favorite food

oya relented and presented him with a gift:
two horns
and a promise -
if ever he beat the horns together
she would rush to his aid

---

* *akara* - fried bean balls

eshu the king

eshu wished to rule ijebu ode
so he strode into town one day
disguised as a rich tourist
and persuaded the king to let him spend the night in the palace
he got a royal reception just like that

before he retired for the night he entrusted the king with
                                        a wooden box
claiming its contents were invaluable
while everyone slumbered eshu set the palace ablaze
and as the thatched roof burned he raised an alarm
but much of the palace was destroyed by the flames
including eshu's precious box

he claimed it had contained a large fortune and compensate him
                                        the king must
but the sum he named was way beyond the king's means
eshu raved and ranted over his loss
and forced the poor king to surrender his throne
so that eshu got to be king of ijebu ode

eshu the liar

eshu resolved to raze the palace of a king who didn't sacrifice
                                        to him
so he approached the king's forsaken wife
with an offer she couldn't refuse:

"bring some hair from the king's beard
and i'll give you something to make you his favorite wife"

next he sidled up to the king's heir
who-ruled his own realm and had his own palace
eshu told him:

"the king wants to go to war tonight
and he wants you and your warriors to meet him at the palace
now"

finally eshu slunk away to see the king whom he told:
"beware of one of your younger wives -
she's plotting to dispatch you to your ancestors tonight"

the king feigned sleep in the night and saw his wife steal in
she only wanted to snip off some hair from his beard like
                                    eshu told her to do
but the king fearing she was after his life
sprang up and plucked the knife from her grasp

a fierce argument followed and behold
their son came in with his soldiers like eshu told him
he saw the king holding a knife and arguing with his wife
who was the prince's mom
the king thought his son was about to unseat him
and in the resulting mayhem many people died

eshu the mischief-maker

two friends always dressed in identical clothes
went around together like needle and thread
for they vowed to stay friends for as long as they lived

now ifa advised them to sacrifice to eshu
but the friends declined
so eshu determined to break up their famous friendship

one day they were working together in the farm
a few hundred metres away from each other
when eshu passed by wearing a bi-colored cap
red on one side and white on the other

one friend asked:
"hey who was that guy in the red cap?"
the other replied:
"it wasn't red - it was white"

they pounded insults back and forth like a squash match
and when eshu passed by once more

the first friend said he realized now the cap was white
the other flew into a rage as he insisted the cap was red
and the two fought fiercely
inflicting grave wounds on each other

when they regained their health and their senses
they obeyed ifa and sacrificed to eshu
and stayed firm friends forever

LAND OF THE LONG HORN

Hausa Myths and Stories

AUTHOR'S INTRODUCTION

Hausa is the second most important language of black Africa; Swahili is the first. The majority of the Hausa are found in Northern Nigeria and the adjoining parts of Niger, but there are several scattered Hausa communities in Burkina Faso, Burundi, Cameroon, Central African Republic, Chad, Congo (Brazzaville), Gabon, Ghana, Guinea, Cote-d'Ivoire, Liberia, Mali, Mauritania, Senegal, Sierra Leone, Togo, Sudan, Zaire, the Maghreb and Medina. However, the Hausa are confirmed travellers and can be found in most of the important towns in West and North Africa.

Hausaland lies between the Sahara in the north and the rain-forests in the south, between Lake Chad to the east and Niger to the west. The Hausa are of mixed origin and present a diversity of features and physiques. They claim descent from a prince of Baghdad who came to Daura and married the Queen after freeing the people from the terror of a giant snake. The couple's children and grandchildren became the founders of the seven Hausa states.

As a result of Arab invasions, the Berbers in North Africa were obliged to emigrate to Hausaland where they intermarried and co-existed peacefully with the indigenous people. The union probably gave rise to the Hausa language and the seven original states or Hausa Bakwai, namely, Daura, Kano, Rano, Katsina, Zazzau, Gobir and Garun Gabas or Biran.

Islam reached Hausaland (Kanem on Lake Chad) in the 11th century but did not exert a strong influence until the 14th century. The Hausa are now among the most devout Muslims in the world.

The Fulani are a different tribal grouping. Often slight and wiry with clear features, they are widely believed to have come originally from North Africa or the Middle East. They are a nomadic people given to moving with their cattle which they cherish highly. There are now groups of Fulani in almost every country between the Atlantic and the Red Sea, but the greatest number live in Hausaland.

About the middle of the 18th century, one of the most influential African men appeared on the Hausa scene, Usman dan Fodiyo, better known as Shehu, the Hausa corruption of Sheikh. He was a Fulani originally from Futa Toro near the Atlantic. He made a name as a Muslim preacher but his austere beliefs caused a clash with the Hausa Chief of Gobir. In 1804, Shehu fled from the threat of persecution and a war later followed, the jihad which he fought for religious reasons. The result was that the Fulani dominated Hausaland for 100 years before they were displaced by the larger numbers of Hausa who imposed their language and customs on them, although the Fulani retained their distinctive look.

The country is a land of plains and very few hills. The early societies before 1500 were simple and self-contained, with men's lives centred around the court and women's around the well. Later, as Islam spread and trade developed, the isolated villages grew into cities, then city-states, states and finally empires. During this latter period, there were six main classes in Hausa society. In descending order, they were the feudal aristocracy and royal bureaucracy, the Mallamai (scholars and jurists, divines), the merchants and craftsmen; the peasants and finally the slaves. However, other divisions such as religious and tribal cut across these classes.

The Chief (or head of administration) was chosen from one dynasty by an independent electoral college. The administration was partly feudal and partly bureaucratic. It was also hierarchical and titles were keenly sought after. The half-veiled, stern-looking chiefs were known as the Galadima; then came the Madawaki, Turaki, Tafida, Dan Galadima, Wambai, Bardes, Ubandoma, Shantali, Ma'aji, Magatakarda, Sarkin Lifidi, Sarkin Doka, Sarkin Dogarai, Yari and others. Each Emirate had its own hierarchy and regulations concerning the bestowal of titles.

Waging wars and slave-raiding were mostly carried out by the Emirs, the nobility and the royal slaves. In the days before gunpowder, battles were fought with lances, javelins and swords borne by the nobility and royal slaves on horseback and with bows and arrows borne by the foot-soldiers. The armies lined up and charged one another across open ground. Towns were fortified by high clay walls, up to 30 feet high. In addition to wars, there were punitive expeditions against vassal states and raids made on pagan tribes.

The Hausa exported slaves to North Africa and the Middle East to source their imports of cowrie shells (local currency), muslin, silk, velvet, salt, copper, needles, horses and chain-mail.

The Malamai were Muslim scholars and divines who settled disputes by referring to the Shari'a, taught the young in Koranic schools and lectured adults in scripture, law, tradition and ritual. They also officiated at weddings and funerals. The majority lived modestly and added to their meagre incomes by making charms and amulets, potions from ink in which the holy texts had been written, and by foretelling the future by tracing designs in sand.

However, there were also the very pious and devout Mallams on the one hand and the worldly and dishonest Mallams who either exploited the ignorance of the common people or practiced black magic. Their influence increased after the jihad and they became the censors of morals. Their power can be seen in "The Sunday Battle" where the Sultan of Sokoto consults them before deciding whether to fight the British in early 1903.

The peasants were often the characters in the stories and they formed the largest audience for the itinerant storytellers.

Physically, the Hausa owe more to their Berber than to their Sudanese ancestry. They are often chocolate-colored and full-lipped and they have narrow hips and strong shoulders although they are not very tall. They have great powers of endurance.

Hausa are less intellectual than practical. As traders, they are realistic and shrewd. They know their stations in society and usually respect those in authority. Arguably, one of their most admirable traits is their easy-going lifestyle which is a result of their great fortitude in the face of adversity.

ADDITIONAL NOTES

(1) Ogres in Hausa folklore are huge and strong men who wear seven-league boots and have tails. They live alone in the deep forest with their human wives who easily deceive them. Although they are not farmers, their stores are always full. They keep goats, sheep and cattle and are skilled hunters of men. However, they are vulnerable to water and often end up being drowned in the Niger or Benue (major West African rivers) where they may then hunt as water spirits.
(2) "Dan-karin-gwiwa" literally means "little cyst on the knee", a name often given to troublesome boys.
(3) Ashanti was the southwestern terminus of a major caravan route which began in Egypt and passed through Hausaland. The Gardawa

are a community of entertainers who specialize in dancing, druming and snake-charming.

(4) The Burmawa were a tribal group which soon became assimilated by the state but were allowed a greater independence than ordinary feudal vassals.

(5) The Sherif Abdur Rahman here is probably Sheikh El-Maghili, a Muslim missionary from Arabia, not a Sherif, who came to Hausaland from North Africa.

(6) The long horn (kakaki) is still used by all the Nigerian Emirs and is a symbol of rank. Ostrich-feather slippers are peculiar to Kano. The Council of Nine (Tara ta kano) were nine leading office-holders.

(7) Both the Hausa and the Fulani attach much importance to signs.

(8) "Haba" is a Hausa exclamation with no English equivalent because the meaning changes with the tone of voice. In "Sokoto's Last Public Execution", the condemned man uses the word to show contempt for the executioner's clumsiness.

Features of African Folklore

They have much in common with one another. They show a certain realism and lack of sentimentality, a possible explanation for the rarity of creation myths. There is a recurrence of aethiological explanations and dilemma situations in which the hero or the audience has to choose between two or more alternatives.

Sources

* H.A.S. Johnson, *A Selection of Hausa Stories.* (Oxford University Press, 1966)
* Frank Edgar, *Litafina Tatsuni yo yi na.* (Hausa, 1913)
* C.E.J. Whitting, *Hausa and Fulani Proverbs.* (Lagos, 1940)
* The First British Resident of Sokoto Province, John Alder Burdon, who collected together with his African assistants, most of the 1 000 stories and 2 000 proverbs which were later published in books edited by Frank Edgar and C.E.J. Whitting.

Land of the Long Horn

Hausa Tales

abuyazidu and the queen of daura

abuyazidu was a prince of baghdad
following a fierce fight with his father
he left home and went west
to bornu in hausaland

there
he married magira
daughter of the sultan
and settled in bornu
where he became a rich and powerful figure

but his good fortune aroused hate and envy
and the sultan plotted to dispatch him to his ancestors

magira the sultan's daughter sniffed out this evil scheme
and promptly notified prince abuyazidu
so although she was hugely heavy with child
they put their possessions on a mule
and with a slave girl in tow
headed west

when they arrived in garun gabas
magira brought forth a son
but abuyazidu rapidly relieved himself of the burden
that was wife and child
and taking the slave girl as concubine
he roamed right on

much later he came to the town of daura
ruled by the last of a line of nine queens

he stayed in old woman waira's home
when in the evening he asked for water

she told him that only on fridays
did daura denizens gather to draw water

abuyazidu dismissed her words with a wave of his wiry hand
and made her get him a bucket
which he took down to the well

sarki the kingsize snake dwelt in the well
and hearing the metallic clang of a bucket
lifted its large head and lunged
at the daring prince
who drew his sword and decapitated it
in one smooth stroke

he hid its head then drew some water
for himself his horse and the old woman
and went to bed

at daybreak
daura residents discovered
the lifeleas snake
they gaped awhile
and then duly informed the queen

she sallied out with all her warriors in tow
and she too marvelled at the massive snake
half of which was still lying inside the well
she vowed she would reward its killer
with the gift of one half of her town

an onlooker right away claimed
it was he who had slain the snake
but the clever queen commanded him to produce its head
as proof

the man did not move his mouth again
and others who made the same mendacious claim
were shown up by their failure to furnish the head

finally old woman waira revealed
that the eve before

a strange man with a huge horse had stayed in her home
and taking her bucket against her advice
had drawn water from the well
for himself his beast and her
it was he - she figured - who had killed the snake

the queen gave orders for this stranger to be found
at once
and he was

abuyazidu admitted he had beheaded the snake
and he produced its head
as proof

the queen was awed
but a woman of her word
and she offered abuyazidu one half of the town

but he would not hear of this division of daura
and said instead he'd be greatly honored
if she consented to be his consort
thus did the prince of baghdad marry the queen of daura

henceforth abuyazidu made his home in daura
where he was bestowed with the title of 'makas-sarki'
or the slayer of the snake –
in time he became simply known as 'sarki'

the concubine he brought from bornu soon bore a son
and believing the queen to be barren
felt sure her son would become chief
so she named him karabgari
or take-the-town

but she was in for a great surprise:
the queen herself soon had a son
whom she called bawogari
or give-back-the-town

eventually makas-sarki and the queen passed on
they were succeeded by their son

140

so bawogari became the first chief of daura
and had six sons:
gazaura the eldest next assumed power
bagaudu the second son became founder of kano
gunguma the third son became founder of zazzau
duma the fourth son founded gobir
kumayau the fifth son founded katsina
zuma kogi the youngest became founder of rano
the son of abuyazidu's first wife magira became
founder of garun gabas
these are the hausa bakwai
the seven original states of hausaland

wari's sacrifice

the *burmawa** of sokoto came to the west
in the time between the death of kanta
and the birth of shehu

when zamfara and kebbi were warring neighbors
the *burmawa* settled in the land between the two foes
and sided with the *zamfarawa**

once when zamfara and kebbi were at war with each other
someone prophesied that the zamfara people would lose
unless a man was sacrificed

on hearing this a burmi man sallied forth
and offered to give his life if his family would be honored
as a result

the deal was done
wari was sacrificed
and the *zamfarawa* won the war
as had been prophesied

so the chief of zamfara bestowed a title on wari's brother ilo:
'sarkin burmi'
a title still used by district heads

141

of the main towns founded by the _burmawa_*:
tureta
bakura
and jabo towns

wari's sacrifice was immortalized
through the _burmawa's_ adoption of the battlecry:
dungun!
all or nothing!
dungun!

---

*_burmawa_ - the people of burmi
*_zamfarawa_ – the people of zamfara

sarkin kano muhammadu rumfa (AD 1463-1499)

muhammadu dan yakubu also known as muhammadu rumfa
was the twentieth chief of kano
and son of a woman from rano called fadimatu

sarkin rumfa was a righteous man
and a scholar as well
kano never had another chief like him

during his reign
abdur rahman and his followers came to kano
it is said the Prophet revealed Himself to abdur rahman
in a dream
with these words:
"arise
go west
and establish islam there."

so he put some dust from medina in his bag
and started his odyssey into hausaland
en route he stopped at every town

then mixed some of its dust with the dust from medina
and if there was no match he moved on

finally he arrived in kano where the dust
matched the medina dust unmistakably
thus abdur rahman recognized kano was the town in his dream

he stopped in panisau
and contacted the chief
who hurried to meet him
and make him and his ten votaries welcome

abdur rahman established islam in kano
using the books he'd brought
to instruct rumfa in matters religious
he built a mosque with a minaret
to replace the *juju** tree he had felled
soon the city was filled with *mallams**
and the state religion was islam

then abdur rahman returned to egypt
having accomplished the task he had been assigned

sarkin rumfa started several things in kano
first he built the palace now called rumfa's palace
then he widened the walls of the city
from the dagachi gate to the mata gate
to the gyartawasa gate
to the kawaye gate
to the naisa gate
and finally to the kansakali gate

next he founded the kurmi market
and in the battle against katsina
he was the first to have spare chargers
brought into battle

he was also the first to take pagan women as concubines
when he sent darman into the slave settlements
with orders to bring him every virgin found there
also he was the first to have a harem of a thousand women

and he was the one who introduced _purdah_*
he also was the first to establish the council of nine
and to bring in _kakaaki_*
the long horn
and the ostrich feather fans and slippers
then too he was the first to use the shadokoko prayer ground
for moslem festivals
and the first to confer titles on eunuchs

truly kano never had a chief to rival him
so a special designation was reserved for him:
'paragon among princes
cleanser of the state'

during his reign they went to war with katsina
for eleven long years
but the war was a draw

in all
he ruled for thirty-seven years

---

* _juju_ - charm or supernatural power in West Africa
* _mallams_ - Moslem scholars and divines
* _purdah_ - system of excluding Moslem women from public view
* _kakaaki_ - long horn used by the Emirs

laughter without end

from the east kanta's father came to hausaland
to settle in katsina
later he became head of his village
and gained the title 'magaji'

he married a hausa woman

who bore him two sons
the first was named kanta

a lively talented child
good at all the usual games
but wilful, violent and rash
so that on his father's death they chose someone else as successor

this made kanta furious and he left
to seek his fortune in the wider world
from katsina he went west
through gobir and zamfara
and beyond western hausaland
beyond the river rima
to the distant village of surame
where he settled down with his allies and aides

sarkin burmi who ruled surame
decided to deal with the wild kanta and his band
by leading some armed men against the lawless herd
but kanta and his gang put up the fiercest fight
massacring all of sarkin burmi's men
while kanta strangled the sarkin with his bare hands

at the end of that brutal and abrupt battle
kanta's troupe addressed him as sarkin burmi
but kanta spurned the title of the man he'd slain
saying he would make his mark in the world
by using his own name

kanta and company then lived in the valley of river rima
a land disputed by the hausa states in the east
and the songhai empire in the west

in 1513 askia the great invaded hausaland
kanta joined forces with him and thus juggled
himself into power

two years after conquering hausaland
askia attacked

the desert state of air
with kanta at his side
and added air to songhai
but dividing the booty broke up the strong alliance
kanta felt he wasn't given his fair share
and he quarrelled with askia

who then sent an army to stop him from seceding
but he repulsed the attack and upheld his independence
in this way kebbi was created
as the last of the hausa states

kanta ruled kebbi for thirty-five years
turning an insignificant state into the supreme power in hausaland

by subduing asben and air in the north
nupe and borgu in the south
zamfara and zazzau in the east
arewa and zaberma in the west
so that all the neighboring states now paid tribute to kebbi
instead of to bornu or songhai as they'd done before
kanta's kingdom stretched from the niger to the sahara
and he managed to keep older empires at bay

he built three capital cities
the last one - surame
he compelled the states that paid him tribute
to provide money and labor
for building surame

when the tuaregs got his goat he penalized them
by denying them water from the river rima which they needed
for their work
he made them take their camels all the way north
just to get water from their own land
when the nupes were late to work he denied them water
saying they must get shea-nut oil from their own country
and mix the mortar with it

he had built a _sirati*_ across a dry moat

it formed a part of the palace and the reason was this:
when he tried a case and had doubts about the accused one's guilt
he would order this person to cross the sirati* a successful crossing
was proof of innocence
but the guilty fell off the bridge
right on to the red-hot embers or razor-sharp stakes
or the wild wild beasts waiting down below
bornu dominated the hausa states of old
and was always at war with kanta
one day a bornu army marched through hausaland
bringing the battle into the *kebbawa** capital and taking its toll
in kebbawa lives

the bornu commander expected consequent victory
but when his men marched up to the walls of kebbi
they found to their alarm that all openings were manned

kanta had fooled them but good
for the defenders were merely dead men propped up
with their lips slit so that they grinned grotesquely at the enemy
scaring them silly
whereupon the bornu army retraced their steps

this event was called dariya ba loto
or laughter without end

the *kebbawa** bounced back and later attacked bornu
under the leadership of the unshakeable kanta
they crushed the kanuri in seven ruthless battles
but on the way back kanta was wounded in a brush
with a minor hausa town
a poison arrow struck him and he died at dan ashita in katsina
his men took his body back to kebbi and buried him there
and the grave is still concealed after all these years

today surame is abandoned but there remain fragments
of the city walls
the palace and even the *sirati**
kanta's well is dry but has not disappeared
and although the silk cotton tree under which he died is no more

there is a gamji tree which is supposed to have grown
from the stake that served as a picket for his horse
on the day that he died

---

* _sirati:_ in Moslem theology the bridge narrow as the edge of a sword
which all must cross after death and from which the wicked fall into
hellfire.
* _kebbawa_: the people of kebbi

sarkin kano alwali and the schoolboy

alwali asked his divines for the name of his successor
so they delved into their deeply guarded secrets
and fished out this answer:

"when alwali leaves the palace the next morning
the first person he sees will be his successor"

as soon as he heard the first cock crow
alwali bounded from his bed
and left the palace through the south gate
but all he saw was a schoolboy in a tunic
clutching a satchel as he ambled around to the eastern quarter
from the west

when alwali told his soothsayers that he had only seen a schoolboy
they asked him to repeat the exercise
so he did and saw the same schoolboy
and still the soothsayers told him to try again
so the next day he did
and saw the same schoolboy

this boy was neither blind nor deaf and certainly not dumb
and he noticed alwali's strange stares
so out of discretion and a sense of self-preservation
he decided that on the following day

148

he would pass by the north gate of the palace
leaving the south gate for alwali the chief

alwali had been hoping to meet a prince or some nobleman
but he kept bumping into the schoolboy
so he told the diviners that for three consecutive days
he had followed their directions and met no one
with the exception of a simple schoolboy

the diviners nodded sagely and said:
"tomorrow go through the north gate instead
and you will see what you will see"

thus it happened that the boy passed by the north gate
on the same day that alwali tried the north gate
and they ran into each other yet again

this time alwali lost his temper completely
and bawled out the poor schoolboy:
"if i catch you passing through the palace gates again
i'll make you one head shorter
you'll see"

the boy shook like a leaf in the eye of a storm
his breaking voice trembled
as with bowed head he cried:
"long may you live
long may you live
forgive o forgive me sir!"

alwali told his soothsayers that he had seen the same schoolboy
and they chorused:
"what will be will be"

events proved them right
the future was as they had foretold
and sulimanu the schoolboy succeeded alwali
thereby becoming the first fulani emir of kano

sarkin kano sulimanu

sulimanu became the first fulani emir of kano
but other fulani leaders prevented him from moving into the palace
because mallam jibir the head of the yolawa clan said
if the fulani lived in the homes of hausas
their children would change into hausas

sulimanu lived instead in sarkin dawaki's home
until the day a kano man said
sulimanu could only be a real ruler if he lived in rumfa's palace

a confused sulimanu sent an s o s to shehu
telling him of the opposition of the fulani leaders
and the admonition from the kano man –
should he move into the palace
or should he stay out?

shebu allowed him to move in
and sent him a sword and dagger to show
he had the power of life and death over his subjects

today every emir of kano gets a sword and dagger
on his appointment
and he keeps these beside him when holding court

sulimanu ruled for thirteen years
during which he worked to strengthen islam
and unify his people
while spurning pomp and splendor

they say that one year during the great festival
he couldn't afford to buy a ram
and the people assembled on the prayer ground
after the sermon
as they waited for the emir to slaughter his own ram

but sulimanu addressed them saying:
"go home and sacrifice your rams o people
the Lord did not provide a ram for my household this year

He doeth what He willeth
and who are we to object?"

they left the prayer ground for the city
and the rich and powerful rushed to press
their fat rams on the emir
who refused every single one
saying he had not told the truth in order to solicit
presents from them

during his reign the councillors lived as simply as he
when the court was in session they went right on
working at their crafts while seated on their mats
they were councillors who led ordinary lives
and didn't suffer from delusions of grandeur
like their latter-day counterparts

the emir himself liked gardening
and at the end of the court sessions
the councillors would roll up their mats and return to their homes
while sulimanu would throw off his court clothes and cry:
"off with kano and on with my garden!"

the fall of zamfara

a long-drawn-out war raged between gobir and zamfara
first zamfara got the upper hand
but the tables were turned abruptly and gobir besieged zamfara
and finally broke into the town

malu the chief of zemfara feared his number had come up
and returning to his palace
he bade his wives strangle him
preferring to die before he was captured by the enemy
so finding no rope
they strangled him with his own turban

barbari the chief of gobir heard of his army's victory
while ensconced in the capital alkalawa

and ordered that malu's head be brought to him
he gloried in getting the gory object
for he felt that the fire down south had finally been put out

long after this
gozo the chief of katsina visited alkalawa
although he was old he travelled a lot
justifying his wanderlust thus:

"it's true that i'm ninety-seven years young
but what else can i do?
there are fewer pleasures left to explore
i've had a good innings and now i'm bored
i no longer enjoy food or women or horses
all i want to do is roam the world
see the world and let the world see me
i'm only ninety-seven and i want to live"

in alkalawa
he found the people of gobir were still crowing over
their victory in the war with zamfara
and he wiped their grins away with these words:

"it's true that you doused the zemfara flames
but beware of a future irrepressible fire"

he was right -
usuman dan fodio was soon to make a momentous entrance

kolanuts for shehu

during the reign of shehu dan fodio
a trader was carrying a caravan load
of a hundred thousand kolanuts
from ashanti to the river niger

when the men, animals and caravan were all safely ferried across
it was the trader's turn to cross

he got in a canoe and as he was crossing
a storm roared and raged and rolled the canoe
so that the poor trader trembled
and called on shehu dan fodio to deliver him from a watery grave

almost immediately
a man emerged in the middle of the river
swung the canoe around
and disappeared

the trader reached dry land
unhurt
and vowed that on arrival in sokoto
he would give shehu ten baskets of kolanuts

shehu was teaching his disciples in sokoto
when suddenly - without any warning - he left
only to return in soaking wet clothes
remarking cryptically that in twenty days they would know why

finally the caravan reached sokoto
and the trader set up camp
then taking five baskets of kolanuts
he went in search of shehu

he informed shehu of his near mishap
and the miraculous rescue
it was then that shehu's disciples realized
why his clothes had been wet

the trader presented the five baskets of kolanuts to him
as an expression of his gratitude for being delivered from drowning
shehu accepted the gift with a rueful smile
saying:
"you haven't kept your promise - ten baskets you pledged
not five."

the trader felt a flush suffuse his face
and returning to his camp he brought
five more baskets

153

which he implored shehu to accept

shebu received the kolanuts and granted his pardon
then shared the offering with his faithful followers
finally he blessed the trader and bid him godspeed

sarkin gobir ali and the butcher's knives

the fulani conquered alkalawa
capital of gobir
they killed the chief
sarkin gobir yunfa
and forced the gobirawa between the devil and the deep blue sea:
either flee up north or be ruled by the dreaded usuman dan fadio

those who fled dispersed to the edge of the desert
and tried to wring a living from the infertile land
leaderless and lawless they stayed there for ten years
after which one of their ex-rulers led a group of them south
where they submitted to sokoto town

bello the new sultan agreed to take them in
letting them settle in the area that had been gobir
and allowing their leader ali to take the title
of 'sarkin gobir'

but far up north were many *gobirawa** rebels
who refused to surrender to the sultan
and they forayed frequently into sokoto
deriding their kinsmen for giving in to the fulani

ali tried to shut the gibes out of his mind
but the cries of 'coward' eventually hit the mark
and fifteen years later an emissary arrived
from the unyielding *gobirawa* in the north

ali was surrounded by his servants
when the messenger came bearing a gift

154

the package was opened and everyone saw
a set of gleaming butcher's knives

the barb struck home
for only the fulani slaves did the lowly work of butchers

this insult led ali to revolt against the sultan
and he returned north to reunite with his kinsmen:
the tuaregs and the katsinawa
both foes of the fulani

sultan bello of sokoto rose to crush ali's revolt
he led an army northeast
across the river rima
till they faced ali's forces at gawakuke

fierce fighting followed
and the tuaregs gave in
while their chief fled from the field

thus the fulani butchered the armies of gobir and katsina
and the dead included sarkin gobir ali and sarkin katsina rauda
leaders of gobir and katsina

when the war ended the fulani ruled
the whole of hausaland
but they never could crush the hausa exiles up north
and sultan bello died two years later

---

*gobirawa - the people of gobir

the death of sarkin kebbi karari

during sultan bello's reign muhammadu hodi fought the fulani
and declared himself thirtieth chief of kebbi
just before he was conquered by the emir of gwandu
and killed

155

consequently
his aged brother karari declared himself chief
and steadfastly fought the fulani
in spite of sultan bello's three calls for submission

sokoto and gwandu rose and rubbled kebbi town because
it sided with karari
and two war years later karari found himself surrounded
in argungu
with no place to go
he and his men were full of fighting spirit
but the people of the town were tired
and yielded
when the fulani fired flaming arrows into their thatched roofs

the city gates swung open
and karari fled with his men
scurrying across the river
to seek refuge in *zazzagawa**

when the fulani pursued them
karari's son yakubu nabame convinced him to run
so he and his army streaked down the north-west road

the fulani followed so faithfully
they were able to eliminate all of karari's men
save two:
karari himself and yakubu his son

now old man karari was heavily hurt
and unable to move
his son believed it was his filial duty to stay at papa's side
but papa had plans for a huge progeny
and he told his son
"save yourself and posterity"

while his son rode away into the future
karari clenched his teeth as he alighted from his horse
stretched out his shield on the rocky ground
and there sat cross-legged

counting his prayer beads
and waiting for death to come calling

it did when the fulani hounds found him
fakon sarki is the name of the spot where he met with his death

---

zazzagawa - the people of zazzau

the rebel

after karari died yakubu nabame went into hiding
for several years
in the province of arewa
but he soon tired of being a fugitive
and in kebbi he surrendered to the fulani

the emir of gwandu sent for his sages
and sought to know if he should slay or spare yakubu
the scholars replied:
"kill him and cause a forty-year drought"

so the emir spared yakubu's life and sent him to sokoto
in this way separating him from the revolt mongers

sultan bello in sokoto allotted a palace-side house to him
where he lived for a long time
a laudable life that earned him
the rank of honorary relative of the sultan

sultan bello's successor had to contend with a *gobirawa** attack
on the town of gora in the sultanate central
he sent umoru his eldest son with a fulani exhibition
to stop the attackers

but not without putting the callow lad in the charge of yakubu

the fulani fought the gobir raiders
and a gobir man taunted yakubu
for aiding his father's killers instead of the gobir side
but yakubu just let the jeering pass over him

the gobir raiders routed the fulani
and umoru the future sultan nearly lost his life
but yakubu saved him
so when they returned to sokoto
the sultan showed his gratitude by offering to grant yakubu
any favor he asked

yakubu sought permission to return to his people
and he did
but while there
he recalled the _gobirawa_* taunt during the fighting in gora
and words which had been simmering now boiled over

so he followed in his father's footsteps
and declared himself chief of kebbi
free from the yoke of the fulani

the emir of gwandu and the sultan of sokoto
seeing yakubu as a traitor
sent an army to clip his wings
but although they surrounded him in argungu
they couldn't take the town or crush the rebellion
and so the kebbawa regained their independence
thanks to the valiant yakubu

---

* _gobirawa_ - the people of gobir

the magician who couldn't save himself

following yakubu nabame's death
yusufu mainsara became the next chief of kebbi
one day in the fifth year of his reign
he received an s o s from gulma town
which was under attack
so he got together all of argungu's horsemen
and they tried to cross the rima valley

but the fulani laid an ambush for him
and hacked his horse down
then because he stood defiant and still
he was killed and his head lopped off
and transported triumphantly to gwandu
where it was stuck onto a stake over the gate facing argungu town

in argungu they chose muhammadu ba'are
nephew of yusufu
as the new chief of kebbi
and after the coronation the council members gave him
this counsel:
"to fend off the fate that befell your uncle
you must move mallam muhamman away from gwandu
at once"

this mallam was a master of the occult
a fulani from the far west
beyond the bend in the river niger
and though new in gwandu
his name reverberated all over the land
so that people in argungu thought that his powers
had sucked their late chief yusufu into the ambush
that proved fatal

the new chief heeded the counsels of his councillors
and he sent secret messages to the magician in the enemy's camp

promises of lush prizes prompted mallam to defect
and he told the emir of gwandu that he wished to go home

159

then headed west thus giving weight to his lie
but as soon as he'd scaled through fulani territory
he retraced his steps back to argungu

when he came to the palace in kebbi
the chief told him:
"mallam
i know you caused my uncle's death
but i will overlook that if you do one thing:
help me to avenge his death on haliru sarkin gwandu"

the mercenary mallam muhamman demanded a reward
so the sarkin kebbi made him an offer he couldn't refuse:
"i'll double haliru's gifts to you –
concubines and cattle
slaves and horses
and everything else
if haliru gave you five
i'll give you ten
and if he gave you ten
well then take twenty!"

mallam muhamman's eyes gleamed with naked greed
as he squealed:
"your highness
you got yourself a deal!"
next the chief suggested laying an ambush for haliru
in gulma or sauwa
large kebbi towns facing fulani fortresses across the rima valley
but mallam muhamman said
"karakara will be a better town for an ambush"

but sarkin kebbi didn't agree
because he said karakara was in the backwoods
and haliru would not be drawn there himself
though he might send an army out

but mallam muhamman insisted
"karakara is where i'll draw him
and you can lay an ambush there"

the chief asked if the mallam would go there himself
but he said that wasn't necessary
as he could work from kebbi
while the chief carried out his own task

mallam muhamman then retired to his residence in the town
where he mumbled charms
and concocted magic spells

in the meantime
the chief sent his premier captains to karakara
to prepare the people for the gwandu raid
defences were arranged
lookouts took up locations
and an ambush was readied

weeks later haliru attacked karakara
and ran right into a brick wall of defense
when he tried to withdraw he fell into the trap
and was butchered just as yusufu had been
with his head hacked off and carried to argungu

the kebbawa revelled in their resounding success
the fulani had been defeated
and haliru was dead
so the chief called mallam muhamman to the palace
and congratulated him

the magician then asked for his pay
and was told to wait until the following day
in the night sarki kebbi held a secret meeting with his councillors
subject:
whether to pay mallam muhamman in full
and grant him an unconditional release

one councillor said
"may your life be long o chief
but this magician may try the same trick twice
we all know a leopard doesn't change its spots –
since this man doesn't know what loyalty means

161

if we free him he'll go to sokoto or gwandu
and may even treat you as he's treated haliru
so let's deal with him while we still have the chance"

another councillor opined:
"may God prolong your life o chief
i agree with my brother there
but we should keep our word
and pay him what we promised
then sort him out"
the other councillors accepted this proposal
so the chief closed the meeting

the next day the goods were delivered to the magician
in his lodgings:
concubines and cattle
slaves and horses
the whole reward

he completed his packing
then went to the palace to say goodbye
the chief wished him well
and ordered zagi akussa to see him and his people across the river

zagi akussa was the chief's personal attendant
tall and extremely strong
he asked the magician to sit under a tree
while the slaves and animals were sent across the river
then he strode up to mallam muhamman
and offered to take him across the river

mallam muhamman declined the offer
he could cross by himself
thank you

zagi akussa said the water was deep
and he was only obeying sarkin kebbi's orders
so saying
he hoisted the mallam upon his shoulders
and waded into the water

when he came to where the water was deepest
he seemed to stumble
and he sank into the river taking the magician with him
people on the bank thought he was rescuing the mallam
but he soon emerged from the water alone
and hurried to the palace to make a report

thus did mallam muhamman follow haliru of gwandu
who in turn followed yusufu of kebbi
to the land of no return
the magician was unable to save himself

the turncoat

the magaji jan borodo was born in fulani land
he grew up in gande
a town in the rima valley between sokoto and kebbi

they say there was famine in the town
when he got married
and as he had no corn to give his wife
he decided to steal some from his father-in-law's store

as he was sneaking into the store that night
he heard strange noises and so made himself scarce
in the morning his wife's father sent him
two bundles of corn

fearing he'd been identified
and ashamed to face his father-in-law
he left gande for good
and crossed the border into kebbi

toga the chief of kebbi engaged him
but being fulani jan borodo was first held in distrust
till his fighting skill slowly dissolved the *kebbawas*'* doubts

his fame as a soldier won him a close friend
in the form of gero the chief's son

consequently jan borodo was made the magaji
in charge of gudale
near the kebbi-sokoto border
and he secured a name as a most valiant soldier
in the border battles

his best-known exploit is his fight with the fulani champion
in his hometown:
the formidable ubandawaki of gande town

opposite numbers in the fighting line
they often clashed and strained to slay each other
but both were brave and shrewd as they come
and for a while it was a ding-dong battle

then the magaji planned an ambush for ubandawaki
he sent some of his horsemen to feign a scuffle in front of gande
when challenged they were to cut back down an established path
then two zaberma grooms would run after them
and on reaching the ambush site
would fall away from the horsemen as if worn-out
and unable to keep up the pace

ubandawaki was drawn into the trap like a fly into a spider's web

when the kebbi raiders invaded their fields
he and a few of his men rode out to stop them
the enemy withdrew according to plan
while the fulani followed in pursuit till the town was way behind
and they straggled like unravelling hemlines

ubandawaki galloping ahead of his men
saw the two seemingly weary grooms fall off the stirrups
of the horsemen who were helping them to escape

since the horsemen galloped like greased lightning
ubandawaki thought he could only catch
the two blundering grooms
and as his own men were riding towards him
he judged it was safe to dismount and seize the enemy grooms

he tried to do so and tumbled into the trap
surrounded and completely cut off
his horse bolted
leaving him with no means of escape
for a while he put up a spirited defense behind his shield
but in the end jan borodo jumped down from his horse
and overpowered him

but he was defiant and did not plead for mercy
so according to the custom he was held down
and his throat slit like a sacrificial ram's
this thrilled sarkin kebbi toga so much
that he asked jan borodo to name his reward

he dared to demand igge's hand in marriage
she was comely and graceful as a gazelle
and already engaged to sama'ila the chief's nephew
but as the chief had promised jan borodo his heart's desire
igge was taken from her fiance
and given to jan borodo as wife

during toga's lifetime jan borodo's fortune soared
he was elevated from head of gudale to head of argungu
the new capital of kebbi
and was given a seat on the chief's council
but on toga's death he was succeeded by sama'ila his nephew
not gero his son

now sama'ila loathed jan borodo to whom he'd lost his girl
and when gero died soon after his father
jan borodo feared sama'ila would make mincemeat of him
so one dark night he fled the town
taking his wife igge and a few faithfuls
and at dawn on the following day he fell at the feet
of the emir of gwandu

in spite of all the misfortune he had brought them
the fulani forgave him and welcomed him back
and for the rest of his life jan borodo plagued the *kebbawa**
like he'd once plagued his own people

years later he was about to set out on a raid
when his cap containing his charms was knocked off his head
he believed this foreboded ill for him
so he sought out his wife and asked her to forgive him
for all the wrong he'd ever done her
and she obliged

magaji dan borodo never returned from that raid
the kebbi warriors slew him and threw his body aside
while they carried his head and heart back to argungu
to his old enemy sama'ila who rejoiced to receive the gory prize

---

* _kebbawa_ - the people of kebbi

sarkin kano abdullahi and the mallam

during sarkin kano abdullahi's reign
a mallam* made his living in kano by copying out the koran

not far from the palace lived an old woman and her slave girl
the mallam liked to visit the old woman now and then
and she would give him kolanuts

one day when the old woman had gone out
the slave girl went to see her mistress's daughter
the mallam came calling and finding no-one home
soon left

there was a party in the home of the old woman's daughter
and the slave returned
to borrow some of her mistress's best clothes
then rejoined the party pronto

the old woman came home
and finding her best dresses all missing
voiced her protest
bringing the neighbors hurrying to her side

she told them her garments had been stolen
and some of the neighbors recalled
seeing the mallam enter the house
but none had noticed the slave girl go in
and so they told the old woman that they'd only seen
the mallam whom she often gave kolanuts

astounded
she ran off to report the theft to the emir
who summoned the mallam at once

he was brought in and accused of stealing her apparel
but he vehemently denied the charge
although he admitted entering the old woman's home

he insisted he was innocent
while the emir declared he was guilty
and threatened to chop off his right hand
unless he returned the woman's clothes

still the mallam denied stealing her raiment
and the emir ruled that his hand be sawn off

the sentence was carried out
and the poor mallam permitted to go home

in the evening of the same day
the slave girl returned from the party
bringing with her the borrowed clothes
her mistress was distressed by this sight
and ran to the emir in great remorse

"may you live long o emir
but we have badly wronged that poor mallam
he is innocent and now he's lost his right hand

167

my slave was the one who took my vesture
unknown to me"

the emir was stricken with such regret
that he withdrew into his private rooms for one week
when he reappeared he sent for the mallam

and said to him:
"mallam
i have done you a grievous wrong
and so i'll give you as compensation
ten of all worldly goods -
ten slave girls and ten slave boys
ten cattle and ten camels
ten asses and ten mules
ten burnouses and ten gowns
ten turbans and ten towns
ten of everything you need"

but the mallam unimpressed
replied:
"sarkin kano abdullahi
you may keep your worldly goods
God and His Prophet will judge between us
i earned a living by copying out the koran
as best i could
thus hoping to reap a reward in paradise
but you have cut off the hand with which i worked
so hold on to your goods
and i'll reserve the reckoning for God"

then the mallam rose and went away
while the emir retired to his private suite
for thirty long days
repenting of his unjust trial
and henceforth he never passed a hasty judgement again

---

* *mallam* - Moslem scholar and divine

sultan abdu and the mallam

abdur rahman the sultan of sokoto selected one of his sons
to rule durbal town
this son was called the yarima

one day the yarima was out riding when he beheld
a girl in a walled compound
by penetrating her family's privacy with his hawk eyes

the daughter of a mallam*
she was delectable and nubile
and caught yarima's lustful eye
so he sent his servants to abduct her

they broke into the mallam's house
and dragged her away to the yarima
when her father found out she was missing
he confronted the yarima
saying:

"o shame on you
yarima durbal
in the name of God and His Prophet
i beseech you
do not defile my daughter
give her back to me"

the yarima yelled in reply
threatening to thrash the mallam for insolence

but the mallam stayed calm as he answered:
"do as you wish
yarima durbal
but mark my words
yarima
as God is my witness
if you deflower my daughter
your virility will vanish forever"

the mallam returned to his house
where he carried out rare rituals
and prayed for God's help

soon the yarima became impotent
and news reached his father in sokoto
the sultan summoned the mallam and asked
if he had made the yarima impotent

indeed he had
the mallam replied
and he told the sultan the whole story

the sultan begged him to reverse the spell
and a handsome reward would be his
the ruler invoked the names of God and His Prophet
but the mallam still refused to oblige him
saying:

"may you live long
o sultan abdu
but the pen as wrote the spell
is dry as an old woman's breasts
and the only way to end the spell
is to return my daughter's maidenhead"

the sultan put away all royal pride
and pleaded with all his might
even offering the mallam a dizzy sum
but all to no avail
the only way to end the spell
was to return the girl's maidenhead

now sultan abdu was a known tyrant
ordering executions for the slightest affront
nonetheless he left the mallam alone
to the surprise of the sokoto people
and the yarima remained impotent until his dying day

---

* *mallam* - Moslem scholar and divine

sarkin zamfara umaru dan mamudu and the gardawa

during a tour of zamfara town a *gardawa** troupe
came to kaura namoda
before dawn the next day they trouped to the chief's house
dancing and drumming and charming snakes

the racket they made roused the chief from sleep
and he growled like a lion with toothache
demanding to know who dared kick up a din
in the wee hours

a servant said it was the *gardawa**
so sarkin zamfara got up to greet the minstrels
whose chief he received in his reception chamber

"so you are the leader of this gifted troupe?"
the sarkin asked umaru dan mamudu

"yes i am sarkin gardi
the chief of gardi
and the leader of this gifted troupe"

then sarkin zamfara sent a servant into the house
to get the capacious calabash

he obeyed
and in compliance with the chief's next command
beheaded sarkin gardi on the spot
popped the head into the calabash covered it with a table mat
and put the calabash in a corner of the room

then sarkin zemfara gave orders for the rest of the troupe
to be invited in
that they may eat their fill of the bloody human head
so as to better entertain his people
with these words and a sickly smirk
sarkin zamfara and his attendants left the reception room

the other troupe members rushed in

171

expecting to be wined and dined
they spied the large calabash in the corner
and sat down to consume the food

first they waited respectfully for their leader to appear
for they couldn't start without him
when after a while he failed to emerge
they lifted the calabash cover

wallahi tallahi! there was their leader's head
so they scattered in sundry directions
each man for himself and the devil take the hindmost

and this is the reason the *gardawa** have never returned
to kaura namoda

---

* *gardawa* – the people of gardi

TRUE HAUSA STORIES

reminiscences of a veteran

in my youth i fought in the kebbi wars
back then both the kebbawa* and the fulani fought on foot
and on horseback too
but the chiefs only fought on horseback
for horsemen were the main attackers
you see

always they carried some armor
coats of mail or quilted armor
even our horses were helped into quilted armor suits
stuffed with kapok and exceedingly light
we also wore helmets and slung rawhide shields over our left arms

as for weapons we carried a couple of javelins in the left hand
also a sword a spear and perhaps a cudgel
but firearms?
rarely ever –
when we horsemen attacked one another we hurled javelins
and then closed in with swords
the cudgels were reserved for crises

when horsemen attacked the foot soldiers
their swift and hefty chargers often broke up
the formation of their foes
and fought the foot soldiers using swords or spears

bowmen often made up the infantry

they fought unencumbered by shields or armor
only leather loin-cloth that let them leap for cover
into houses or trees or bushes
and a brave bowman under attack could wait
until the horseman came into close range
and then he would pretend to shoot –
if his enemy threw up his shield
the bowman would strike swiftly beneath the shield
putting the poison arrow on rapid release

back then a spy would be used to sniff out the foe's defences
and if he reported a chink in their wall
that crack would be the point of attack
through which the enemy could creep in at night
or rush in by day in a daredevil way

but surprise attacks very often failed
for people kept their walls in good repair
moreover the moats were filled with *sarkakkiya** thorn
so dense it defied horse and man
and only the *yan-lifidi** in quilted armor
dared face the foe behind the parapets

while these daring *yan-lifidi* contended with the defenders
the pioneers and sappers could sneak up and get down

unarmed
but with shields to protect them as they cut through the thorn
and carved a hole in the wall

whenever possible the attackers employed fire:
if houses were very near the wall
the enemy fired blazing arrows into the thatch

and the defenders panicked by the resulting flames
deserted their posts immediately
for this reason houses were often built far from the walls

barring fire a battle became a mere duel:
on one side attackers in quilted armor
on the other defenders behind fortified walls
sometimes they pitched red-hot arrows into the quilting
of the _yan-lifidi_
turning horse and rider into huge tongues of flame

the fighting was ferocious to the finish
because each side knew what it stood to lose:
the town would be burnt
the warriors all killed
and their women and children carried away

those were the days
yes those were the days
men were men then and had more to live for
than now
o yes i fought in the kebbi wars
and that was living
that was living all right
now i'm just waiting to join my ancestors

---

* _kebbawa_ - inhabitants of kebbi
* _yan-lifidi_ - dragoons

abdulbaki tanimuddarin tureta

when i was seven
sarkin zamfara sought help with attacking tureta
from the chiefs of gobir, katsina, mefara and kaura

all five sarkin got together in tureta
but couldn't capture the town
so sarkin katsina slyly stated:
"truly sarkin zamfara has fooled us all
bringing us here to fight against you
but we are brothers o people of burmi
and i shouldn't be here o i shouldn't be here"

we were moved by his words and we called a truce
cooked some food and took it outside the town
while for three days we held peace talks

all of a sudden we saw our town burning –
the enemy fell upon us
and i was taken prisoner along with others

they took me to a place called cikaji
and there i stayed for two dreary years
before my old father found me

prior to my imprisonment someone prophesied
that i would be sarkin burmi one day
but only after experiencing a myriad tribulations –
this prophecy was oft repeated to papa's hearing
and maigunya his younger brother remembered this

now back to the story of cikaji
i was there as a prisoner of war
till my father found out and sent some men to ransom me

they came to the house of dantata my master
but they needed twenty thousand cowries to complete the ransom
so it was decided we'd go to tureta with one of dantata's men
and pay the balance to him

agreement made
we went to bed
but in the night one of dantata's men convinced him
to keep me captive
till the full ransom had been paid
because he claimed my people would first pay their man
then follow him into the forest and kill him there

came the morn and dantata reneged
on his agreement to set me free
insisting every penny be paid
before my people could take me away
so my father's men left me behind
to return at harvest time
if God so willed

i was stuck in cikaji as a suffering slave
while waiting for harvest time to arrive
my father's men were given a favorable date of departure:
the seventh day of the month
and uncle maigunya remembering the prophecy about me
said he would go before them to cikaji
they tried to persuade him to wait until the seventh

but the second was his own lucky date
when he came to cikaji my master was out
and he met kishalli my master's younger brother
who said dantata was in the bush somewhere
then he asked for me
and kishalli fetched me

our meeting only lasted a moment then i was returned to my cell
and when dantata returned
my uncle met with him and his brother kishalli
and told them my father's men would arrive in a few days' time
to pay the rest of the ransom
at which time dantata was to show them a freshly-dug grave
and say i was buried there
having just died before my uncle arrived
my father's men would weep a little and leave

then dantata could sell me to itinerant traders
thereby reaping a double profit

days later rafi and another man came from tureta
and paid the rest of the ransom
one of dantata's men received it reluctantly and said
it was useless to try and hide your navel at bathtime
and the truth was that i abdulbaki was dead

then they took rafi to the empty grave
and he, believing their lie, cried with his companions
and went back home

dantata's men took me from my hiding place
and sold me to tuaregs who were passing by
and that's how i ended up in dadin town
miles away from the civilized world

there bubakar my new master tested me in the tuareg style
by giving me an old ewe to use as i wished
God doeth as He pleaseth
nd He multiplied my ewe
my herd grew and grew
into fifty sheep, twenty-five cattle and three camels
and ten asses besides

my father had become chief of tureta by now
and his friends reminded him of the prophecy
certain that i was still alive though far away
but this only resulted in arguments
and they would send for rafi to confirm
he had indeed seen my grave in cikaji

sarkin kiyawa wished to buy my father's famous bay
but my father refused to take any money
all he wanted in exchange for his horse
was information regarding my whereabouts

sarkin kiyawa wasted no time
he sent men out to seek me
they found someone they thought was me

but when they took him to my father in tureta
it turned out to be my cousin abdu kabau
still my father promised to pay a thousand for him
while sarkin kiyawa's men continued to search for me

i was slaving away in dadin kowa
when my master summoned me one day
and told me i was free to leave
but i couldn't take anything with me
in reply i said nothing

then the next morning i took the animals out
and returned in the afternoon in a foul mood
my master heard the animals bleating
and demanded a reason for my early return

i told him that i hadn't felt like leaving before
but now i was ready and raring to go
i picked up my quiver and water bottle
strapped them on in silence
and flounced out
but he ran after me and grabbing my arm
called for hammado in his native tongue

hammado rushed in and clutched my left arm
so that my quiver slipped to the ground
i was in a fluster as i stooped to pick it up
and made myself disappear
using my infallible _layar zana*_ charm

then i sneaked off to my friend tanko's house
all of thirteen miles away
as you know, every tuareg lives in his own hamlet
away from other tuaregs -
i told tanko about my dispute with bubakar
and asked him to prepare some provisions for me

in the backwoods of dadin kowa
my action had momentarily stunned hammado and bubakar
but being master trackers like all tuaregs are
they trailed me all the way to tanko's house

his wife was pounding corn outside
when she spied them and called out to me
so i slipped into tanko's hut and into his bed
and quickly covered myself with his clothes

bubakar arrived and asked tanko where i was
but my friend denied ever having seen me
bubakar was unconvinced
so tanko invited him to search the house

hammado and bubakar burst in
and did a thorough inspection
of the bean bin and the corn store
tanko's hut and his mother-in-law's
then under the bed
but they didn't find me

they left in a huff
and tanko pledged he'd put bubakar in a pickle –
he told his wife to pound some corn
which he poured into a goatskin bag
then he provided me with a pumpkin
and pulled me after him

we scurried off to tessawa
and duly greeted the chief
then tanko told him i'd been stripped of all my assets
cattle camels sheep and asses
that sprang from my original ewe
the chief listened increduously
but tanko assured him it was all true

next we were taken to the french commandant
and tanko told him how i'd been wronged
straightaway he sent a constable to go with us
and repossess all my animals

the constable worked himself into a frenzy:
his face twitched and froth gathered around his mouth
and he was now ready to confront bubakar

179

when we got there he gave bubakar a good strong shove
and asked if he recognized me
bubakar confessed that he did
and the constable cursed a right blue streak

"you no-good uncivilized dumbbell
can't you see that times have changed?
you can't eat this year's dumplings with last year's gravy
and slavery is plainly out
besides you robbed this man in broad daylight
now return his stock right away
or i will tie you up and tow you to tessawa!"

hammado and bubakar knew he meant business
so they took us to the fields where i picked out
all my cattle and camels and asses and sheep
we took the animals to tanko's house
then accompanied the constable to tessawa
where we reported recovery of my stock
and paid the compulsory court fees

tanko and i then returned to his house
where i joined a group of udi shepherds going south to hausaland
and we bid each other goodbye

there was little trust between the shepherds and me
so i never let on that i didn't know my way home
as all the time they were trying to steal my stock
while day in day out we trekked on
when they weren't looking i would ask the farmers for directions
to tureta

then i would say we should go that way
because water and grazing were plentiful there
now udi shepherds only care about feeding their animals
and so they followed me all the way to fara town

in fara town i told them we'd go our separate ways
but they stoutly refused to let me leave
smelling trouble i stepped aside to arm myself –

my poison arrows told them not to mess with me
for they knew if i killed them i would take over their flock

alone with my animals i went
from fara through dambo, bakura and binasa
stopping to ask for directions all the way
until i reached tureta at long last
God doeth as He pleaseth always

at the entrance to the town i met uncle maigunya
neither of us recognized the other
he had become chief but had since been dethroned
i asked after my father the dangaladima almusdafa
and was told he had joined our noble ancestors

i entered tureta and sent word to the chief
and soon people came rushing out to meet me and all my animals
in the town square
suddenly i heard someone say i looked like abdulbaki
my father's dead son

the excitement attracted my mother and my two elder sisters
who had been told a *ba'ude** had come to town
mama recognized me and almost hugged me to death
saying here was her little abdulbaki returned
and that she had never believed i was dead
wallahi, the merrymaking in tureta that day!

i know that God is the Almighty
Who doeth as He pleaseth
and His will holds sway
even if the odds are stacked against you
if He pleases He will elevate you
behold i am living proof of this truth

---

* *ba'ude* - person of rank or importance

181

the death of captain moloney

i was born near the kofar kokona in keffi
tumbudi the barber was my father and he died when i was twenty
then i was taken in by dan ya musa
the magaji of keffi
because of my friendship with ladan his son

two years after i entered the household
captain moloney arrived in keffi
just before the rains

the magaji was five feet two inches tall
neither fat nor slim
he sported a black beard
and a good set of teeth

he was dark for a fulani and of indeterminate age
and skilled in hunting, horse-riding and fighting
also short-fused
and so virile he had four wives and concubines galore
the most powerful man in keffi was the magaji
not the emir of zaria
although he supervised keffi on the emir's behalf

the magaji's main pursuit was war
in the dry season he always fought
against the toni pagans of dari, amba and riri
and the mada pagans south-east of his headquarters in kokona

magaji dan ya musa saw slaves as lucre
in exchange for trousers, gowns and kola nuts
and the horses from the north to be ridden by his men

the first we heard of the europeans was from a group of tijani
who had been driven from their country by the french
and moved to bauchi

so back to our subject: captain moloney

or "mai launi" as we all knew him
he came two years after i'd been with the magaji
and ordered that war and slavery would have to end
there and then
because he moloney was now in charge
as you can guess the magaji was rattled
for slavery was his livelihood

now moloney had arrived with a man called webster
or mallam bature as we all knew him
two months after their arrival
many soldiers came to keffi
and went with moloney to fight against abuja

they routed the town taking the chief captive
and arrested the robbers and bandits too
but moloney was wounded in the leg
and henceforth he was carried in a hammock

webster had remained in keffi meanwhile
worming himself into magaji's affections
he was always with us in kokona
wallahi i even liked him myself!

moloney also had a chief government agent:
andu timtim
whom i did not like
for he was a liar and a scoundrel
playing moloney off against the magaji

the war with abuja did not last long
and moloney brought some soldiers back to keffi
while others went to lokoja
although mutual suspicion between moloney and the magaji grew
webster remained a trusted ally

one day the magaji went to keffi
and the next day was summoned by moloney
but the magaji sent his excuses
he had a bad case of scabies you see

well two days later
on friday third october nineteen-o-two to be precise
moloney left his rest house in town -
while some soldiers guarded his quarters
others went with him
carrying him in the hammock to the emir's palace
audu timtim and another messenger called musan gana
also accompanied him

from the maga~i's compound a few metres
away i saw them enter the emir's palace
in front of which was a square
the emir's house on one side
the magaji's on the other

soon the emir and moloney emerged
the captain had climbed out of his hammock
and was hobbling alongside the emir
they put a chair out for moloney
while the emir sat down on a mat
and people gathered round to watch

webster was at moloney's side
and their soldiers stood near the emir's gateway
now a messenger was sent to summon the magaji
who did not come
although webster went twice to try to fetch him

noon came and still he would not come
so the emir sent yet another summons
and still the magaji refused to come
moloney wanted to go and fetch him
but the emir would not hear of it
webster was sent a third time to the magaji
who finally emerged on his war horse
followed by soldiers of his bodyguard
and all the time i was watching with other footmen
from the entrance to the magaji's house

he rode across the square towards the emir

but he didn't give the emir the usual spear salute
suddenly i heard a shot being fired
but couldn't tell whence it had come
now i knew the magaji always carried two pistols
and one of them contained six bullets
one pistol he carried under his left armpit
and the other in a pouch on his right hip

moloney had been shot and he fell off his chair
then the people started screaming
and the soldiers started shooting
webster retreated into the mosque
audu timtim ran towards the quarter guard at moloney's house
while the magaji warned against harming mallam bature

one of the magaji's men shot an arrow into the emir's right foot
and chaos held sway in the square
moloney's soldiers were shooting at the magaji
but miraculously they all missed him
while bullets rained down on the confounded crowd

the magaji swung his horse round and rushed after audu timtim
overtaking him under a baobab tree
and ripping out his bowels with his fighting stirrups

this happened not very far from where i stood
and i saw adamu maidoka's slave slice off audu timtim's head
someone else severed moloney's head
and threw it in a well outside the gate of the mosque
later the well was sealed up on the emir's orders

the soldiers now rushed after the magaji
and we ourselves scurried off to kokona
the magaji first galloped to keffin shanu
ten miles away
where he cut the telegraph wire with his sword

then wheeled round to the north and rode beyond kokona
there he disconnected the telegraph wire to lafia
and called in his cattle from keffin shanu and hadari

before returning to kokona and us

he gathered us all together and said
today he'd dug his own grave
and we should leave if we wished
or stay

many remained for old times' sake
and three days later the emir sent a warning:
keffi would be destroyed and myriads of women, children
and infirm killed
unless the magaji left the town at once

the next morning the magaji prodded us awake with his gun
as he did whenever he wanted us to make haste
again he said those who wished could stay behind
and those who wished could go with him to kano
as there were now europeans in zaria

more than a hundred men went with him
plus some forty women, seventy horses and six herds of cattle
and some kano men to serve as guides

first we went to akwanga and then to kachiya
where we met some hunters who helped us to avoid zaria
and the europeans
and twenty-five days later we arrived in kano

the emir sent his men to meet us and usher us in
we were all warmly welcomed
and presented with houses, cattle, rams and food

---

* *Wallahi* - Wallahi Tallahi is an oath similar in meaning to "by
God"

Source: *Concerning Brave Captains* by D.J.M. Muffet, London, 1964.
The narrator is a Hausaman called Hassan Keffi.

the shamaki and the majidadi

one afternoon the british appeared in sokoto
capital of the fulani empire
where they collided with the sultan's men in a minor battle
and some lives were lost

one of the waziri buhari's slaves was killed
so the shamaki rode out alone against the british force
knowing it was a suicidal mission

sleep was scarce that night
for men rallied from all around
and sharpened their weapons
in readiness for war

another slave of waziri buhari's
the majidadi babadarai
was among the crowd
and was seeking his friend the shamaki
when he learned the shamaki was dead

the majidadi was devastated by this news
how could his friend have gone before him to God?
he prayed all night
performed his ablutions and donned a new gown
before dawn

in the morning when the battle was about to begin
the majidadi waited for the enemy to advance
then riding up to the sultan of sokoto he demanded
the goron yaki
or kola nuts of war
as a sign of his intention to die in the war

he received the kola nuts
and while his squire preceded him on foot
he followed on his horse to face the british
but just before he reached the dividing line
he commanded his squire to turn back and save himself

187

the squire refused to heed his master
saying he had always run in front of the majidadi
and *wallahi** he would continue to do so even if it meant
entering the next world
so both men marched into the machine gunfire
and were consumed

---

* *Wallahi Tallahi!* - a Hausa oath meaning "by God!"

the sunday battle

i was nearly thirty when the british came to sokoto
and i inherited the title of "majasirdi" from my father
who was a slave in the sultan's household

for some time we had suspected
the british would attack us
but we in sokoto had made no defence plans
for sultan abdu had died a few months ago
and sultan attahiru was still finding his feet
so he and his council could not decide
how to react to governor lugard's message –
should sokoto fight or make peace?

the sultan summoned all the mallams from the surrounding regions
and asked them what was to be done
the mallams said to fight the british
and defend the faith against infidels

sultan attahiru took the mallams' advice
and began to prepare for war
but at that stage we had already lost bida, kontagora and zaria
and later kano
so we were cut off from the other emirates to the east

there was no time for the sultan to summon help

from gwandu, katsina, yeuri, dawa and kazaure
or even from distant districts of sokoto

on saturday we were expecting the british to attack
so we all came out and marshalled our forces on the city's outskirts
but there was no attack and when night came
we returned to the city to ready ourselves for the following day

on sunday we drew up the line of battle once more
with three divisions –
the marafa maiturare's men on the right
sarkin rabah ibrahim's on the left
and the center was under the sultan
who positioned himself beneath a fan palm tree
while beside him was the sa'i of kilgori

the ground was as bare as the *sahara**
except for the fan palm tree where the sultan was stationed
but beyond the common was some farmland that shielded
the enemy from our view

the british started shooting so the sultan sent five slaves
to spy on them
we were sarkin dawaki, sarkin rakuma, gulbi, tirai and me
but we were blinded by gunsmoke
and the dust from the heels of horses and men
also the noise of the shooting unnerved our horses
and checked our advance
so we were thrown off-course and ended up
on sarkin rabah's front

eventually i managed to get back
to the sultan's quarters
but he was no longer there
i heard the whole story later -

the marafa was a skilled soldier
and had realized that our horsemen were no match
for the enemy's guns
so he'd rushed to the sultan and pressed him to withdraw

entreating him not to let the torch go out while
he was holding it
meaning that if the sultan continued
he'd be staking the survival of sokoto and the shehu's line

the sultan dismissed this with an angry sneer
claiming he had fought other battles before
when the marafa mounted his horse once more
it was shot from under him at once
he mounted another horse which was soon shot down
and then he himself was shot in the shoulder

in the meantime the battle began closing in
on the sultan beneath the fan palm tree
when the sa'i umaru and his soldiers had all been struck down

by machine-guns
the waziri buhari told the sultan that from then on
the blood of the slain would be on his head
this remark made the sultan leave the battlefield

so i returned to his quarters to find him and his bodyguard gone
but the dead were clustered around the foot of the fan palm tree
and i saw my own father in the pile
no my friend don't feel sorry
his days were fulfilled weren't they?

Sahara - desert in North Africa

dan makafo and the satiru rising

at the turn of the century there lived a man
in zaberma
his name was mallam shu'aibu alias dan makafo
so named because he was small and blind

he was a little educated
and passed himself off as a pious man

in reality he was a clever trickster
who claimed to produce kola nuts from the empty air
and lift himself upon his prayer-mat
in this way bamboozling the people into believing
he had superhuman powers
and in spite of his blindness
they held him in much awe

the french invaded kaberma
and sent tax-collectors round to collect tributes
when they came to dan makafo's town
he encouraged the people to attack and kill them

the french responded by routing zaberma
but the conflict cost the lives of two french officers
and a myriad *zabermawa**
while dan makafo fled eastward to sokoto

now seventeen miles south of sokoto
was the small town of satiru
where a year or two earlier an elderly mallam had declared
he was the *mahdi**
but the sultan had arrested him
and he had died in detention
while his son mallam isa lived on in satiru
and the residents retained their mahdist creed

from zaberma dan makafo fled to satiru
where he dazzled the residents with his magic
so that his influence soon rivalled mallam isa's
but the wily dan makafo made him an ally not a foe
and at the beginning of nineteen hundred and six he proclaimed
that he was the mahdi*
and isa was Jesus

the satiru people were pleased to hear this
but in tsomau village nearby
lived mallam yahaya
who had received religious lessons from isa
and was related to him by marriage
but mallam yahaya had rejected mallam isa's claim

on the ground that they'd all known isa as a child

soon the festival of id el kabir came round
and instead of celebrating it in satiru
mallam yahaya and his family stayed away

in revenge
dan makafo and isa sent some men to invade tsomau
the village was carbonized
and eleven men and one woman were killed
including mallam yahaya whose throat was slashed like a ram's

early the next morning the people of satiru learned
the british resident was on his way from sokoto
with troops in tow

so dan makafo and isa rallied their supporters
and hid them in the ground
northwest of the town
almost at sunrise the troops appeared on the high ground
up north
then marched on to the satiru plain
and stopped
while a small group of two europeans and two africans
rode forward alone

when the group came close
dan makafo and isa ordered their men to emerge and charge
but the horsemen stood firm
and the british resident yelled something
that was translated into hausa
by one of the africans in his group
but dan makafo's rebels routed the resident's troops
even taking the resident captive
while the rest were either slain or chased away
and the machine-gun confiscated and carried back triumphantly
to satiru

the rebels knew how deadly the machine-gun could be
but they didn't know how to operate it

so they offered hillary the resident his life
in exchange for teaching them to work the weapon of war

but hillary would not co-operate
and neither their offers nor threats could make him
change his mind
so the rebels began to mutilate him
first hacking off his left hand and then his right
next cutting off both of his feet
then his arms and legs
and they kept on chopping till he died

the rebels also had their casualties
including mallam isa who died of a war wound
leaving dan makafo as the sole leader
but news of their victory drew criminals and other scum to satiru
in search of power and plunder

on the day after isa died
marafa maiturare led the sultan's forces against satiru
once more
and though the marafa fought fearlessly
his men believing the stories about the rebels' magic powers
were easily checked
and the rebels' egos were boosted by this second success
causing them to believe in their invincibility and great destiny

while isa had lain dying he'd prophesied
he would rise again and return to the world
an older prophecy had said
the people of satiru would go into their kingdom
whenever a black bull was seen in their mosque

soon after the marafa's failed attack
a herd of cattle containing a black bull was passing by the town
dan makafo heard of this and acted instantly –
he sent some of his supporters to secretly steal a bull
so they slew the fulani herdsman and when night came
they drove the black bull into the mosque

in the morning dan makafo declared

the bull was the reincarnation of isa
and now the people would enter into their kingdom
as per prophecy

the population of satiru was swelled by outcasts from all around
and so food grew scarce
then dan makafo scared the city's neighbors
into providing his men with food
by giving hillary's shin and thigh bones to the village heads
as presents to serve as pickets for their horses
to frighten them further he also attacked
dange and danchadi nearby
and razed them to the ground
taking the women and children as slaves
and murdering those men who did not become mahdists and rebels

satiru was a wide-open and unwalled town
and yet dan makafo did not fortify the town
he was awaiting reinforcements before attacking sokoto
and in the meantime gave his main henchmen titles –
waziri, galadima and magajin gari
but in the absence of discipline and order
the rebels only danced, drummed and minstrelized
and despite the prohibition of alcohol
they got drunk on a brew made from gawo tree bark

unknown to the rebels who were busy being inebriated
the british troops were on their way
and twenty-four days after the first battle
they invaded satiru with two machine-guns and one field-gun
at the scene of the first war they stopped and formed a square
then the infantry drew the rebels on to the machine-guns

spurred on by an unarmed mallam
waving some paper above his head
the rebels stormed the square vigorously
as the first shots roared from the machine-guns
they shouted in scorn "nothing but beans!"
and then to their surprise
they were being cut down in scores

although their illusion of invincibility was so rudely dispelled
the rebels fought bravely on
at first they were driven back into town
but they would not surrender
so the troops attacked the town with a bayonet
the battle raged for three houra
and the rebels were hunted until nightfall

the troops lay in wait for dan makafo
but the rebel leader managed to elude them
the sultan ordered the whole area combed
and three days later he was captured together with the boy
who served as his guide
and the two were taken to sokoto

there dan makafo was tried for murder and rebellion
in the sultan's court –
at one point the rebel leader asked for some water
but before the sultan could grant his request
the boy being tried with him cried
"if you let him drink he'll just disappear
and then i'll be the only one left!"

as a result dan makafo was denied his drink

he didn't try to defend himself
and was sentenced to death
they took him from the sultan's palace to the market-place
where a mammoth crowd was waiting
but his reputation had reached such incredible proportions
that many still believed he would disappear
or change himself into an animal
or in some way cheat the executioner

but mallam shu'aibu alias dan makafo was as mortal as
any other man
his head was chopped off with just one blow
and stuck on to a stake for all to see

---

* *zabermawa* - the inhabitants of zaberma
* *mahdi* return of Imam Husayn, awaited by disciples of Shi'ih Islam

the last public execution in sokoto

around 1929
the sultan's court sentenced three men to death for murder

they were taken from prison at noon
and marched to the market-place by guards

where
they were met by the presiding officials:
the constable
the market magistrate
the executioner and his assistants

next the doomed men were walked round the market-place
for everyone to see
finally they were led to the execution area
surrounded by a myriad spectators

in those days beheading by sword was the method of execution
and the condemned person was made to kneel on the ground
with his arms tied behind him and his neck stretched out
then the executioner's assistants would divert his attention
by walking before him and drawing a sword
and right away the executioner who would be standing behind him
to one side
would take a step forward and sever his head
to his surprise

but this method could not be used when there were more than one
condemned
and in this case there were three
with hands tied behind their backs
and kneeling in a row

suddenly the mob became still
like a congregation engrossed in silent prayer

all three men showed supreme self-control
as they stared placidly ahead

while the executioner
burly and bare from the waist up
strode toward the first man and struck his head off
with one blow

and now the crowd commenced moaning
but the two other condemned men did not move

then the executioner advanced toward the second man
and sliced off his head with a single stroke
again the crowd released a long low groan
but the third man just stood aloof

now the executioner strode forward to finish his task
this condemned was built like an ox
a brawny fellow with broad shoulders and a bulging back
the executioner's sword missed the target this time
tearing into his back and shoulders to open up a deep wound
which sprayed blood as soon as the sword was removed

the crowd gasped but the condemned man remained calm
turning his head and looking the executioner up and down
as if his fly were open
then the doomed but defiant man spat out in contempt:
"haba!

can't you do better than that?!"

then he turned his head around to the front
and stretched out his neck
to receive the final stroke

---

* *haba* - a Hausa interjection signifying contempt, disapproval, or
surprise

HAUSA FAIRY TALES

the girl and the ogre

she was an only child
and the prettiest girl in town
the honey around which
young men gathered like bees

other girls were so jealous
they plotted to dispose of her
and one day they invited her
to gather firewood with them

she told them her mother was angry with her
and would they ask mother to permit her to go?

they tried but the mother said
her daughter had to pick over some guinea corn
and separate some cotton
then she could go with them

the girls eagerly did all the drudgery
then they went with beauty into the woods
when they came to an ogre's well
they squabbled over who would go in and draw water
each girl saying she couldn't leave her little sister
but beauty was an only child and couldn't offer
the same excuse
so the others decided
she must go down the well

they tied their wraps together
and lowered her into the well
she drew water and they drank till they were satisfied
and then untied their wraps and went away
leaving the poor girl at the bottom of the well

on arrival they were asked
the whereabouts of so-and-so

but they claimed not to have seen her
saying she had abandoned them

soon after they had deserted beauty
the ogre came to his well to water
his camels, cattle, goats, horses, mules, donkeys and sheep
but when he let down his bucket the girl grabbed it
and he begged her to let go
with a promise that he'd pull her out
after watering his animals

now the ogre was a mountain of a man
supremely strong
with eyes like lumps of red-hot coal
and a tail
he wore seven league boots
and lived all alone in the woods
but needed a woman to keep house for him
so he could go hunting men

he fished her out and listened to her story
then asked her to choose between being eaten and married
but she told him that he knew best

so he decided to make her his wife
and got his barber to shave off her hair
next he gave her silver bangles and things
and then named her tamajiro

the ogre was an able hunter
he would dry and store the meat of all that he killed
he set aside a storeroom for human flesh
another one for animal flesh
and yet more storerooms
for eggs, beans, rice and wheat
millet, guineacorn and tiger-nuts
and he gave her free access to all the storerooms

they lived together as man and wife
and she bore him two children

while back home her mother had another child
a son this time

when he was older he told his parents he knew
he had a sister and meant to find her
they told him she was dead
but they couldn't dampen his determination

he planted a pumpkin seed at the back of the yard
and said
"duma
lead me to my sister
wherever she may be"

with the passing of time
the pumpkin plant grew
spreading all over the place
from the yard to the ogre's well
and on to the ogre's house
over the roof of his hut
and into the branches of his _cediya_ tree

one day the boy bid his parents goodbye
"_inna* baba*_
please forgive me for any wrong i have done to you
but now i must find my big sister"

they told him she was dead
but the boy intended to find her
dead or alive
and he set off with the pumpkin plant as guide
it led him to the ogre's well
and into his yard
there he hid himself in the _cediya_ tree

soon his sister came out to crush some corn
so he let a leaf fall into her mortar
and when she picked it out
he repeated his leaf-dropping two more times
until she looked up and saw him in the tree

he came down and talked with her
and she told him she must hide him from the ogre
to save his life

and then she hid him in the tiger-nut store

when the ogre returned from his hunting trip
he sat down to rest
but then sprang up like a lion about to leap on its prey
and declared
"tamajiro
I smell a man!"

she denied that any man would come
where he was sure to be eaten
but the ogre insisted he could smell a man

the girl told him the only human he smelled
were her and their children
and surely he wouldn't eat them would he?

this silenced him
but suddenly he heard a sound from the storeroom
and thinking it was a rat eating the tiger-nuts
he wanted to kill it at once

but she knew it was her brother
and told the ogre she would take care of the rat herself

the boy had heard the ogre growl
and he lay low till the ogre had gone to sleep

in the morning the ogre went out to hunt
and the girl gave her brother half of the ogre's animals
to take home

when he met the ogre along the way
pounding the ground with his club
she advised him to say
"dodo, dodo

husband of tamajiro
killer of men
o let me pass"

so the boy sallied forth with the animals
and in the middle of the woods he saw the ogre far away
eyes as fiery as the light from a blow torch

the ogre espied him too
and pounding the ground with his club
said
"this one is like tamajiro
his eyes, his head, his hands
are like hers"

and then the ogre danced up and down
the same distance as from kano to zaria

he danced away and danced back again
but by then the boy had gone far ahead

the ogre caught up with him
and still pounding the ground with his club
he cried
"is tamajiro known to you?"

the boy repeated the chant his sister had taught him
"dodo, dodo
husband of tamajiro
killer of men
o let me pass"

the ogre replied as he'd done before
"this one is like tamajiro
his eyes, his head, his hands
are like hers"

and then he cut a caper once more
dancing a distance the same as from kano to mecca
he danced away and danced back again

but by then boy and beasts were across the river niger
home and dry
as he drew nearer home
the dust from his animals frightened his people
and they thought an army was marching on their town

back at the ogre's house the girl prepared to follow
in her brother's footsteps
she gathered all the ogre's household goods
the rest of his animals as well
then she swathed herself all over save for a bit of face
and set out for her home town

in the middle of the woods she met the ogre
his eyes glowed like lumps of red coal
and he pounded the ground with his club
then asked
"woman, is tamajiro known to you?"

she answered as she had advised her brother
"dodo, dodo
husband of tamajiro
killer of men
o let me pass"

the ogre replied as he'd done before
"this one is like tamajiro
her eyes, her head, her hands
are like hers"

and he danced off again
the same distance as from zaria to mecca
he danced away and danced back again
but by then the girl had safely crossed the niger
taking along his animals and goods

as she drew near home the people feared
an army was marching upon them
then they saw the girl and were amazed to find
it was old so-and-so come home

from the ogre's well to a triumphant return

the chief divided the town into two
the girl ruled one half
and her brother the other

when the ogre got home he found
his beautiful wife was gone for good

he rushed after her in a wild rage
but too late - she got clean away
the angry ogre fell into the niger and drowned
and now all ogres live in the water

---

* _Inna_ - Hausa word for "mother"
* _Baba_ - Hausa word for "father"

no-lord-but-God

once there was a man called no-lord-but-God
when other men went to the palace
they greeted the chief saying
"may your life be long"
but this man said instead
"there is no lord but God"

this made the chief angry
so one day he sent for no-lord-but-God
and handed him a ring like no other in town
to hold until he wanted it back

no-lord-but-God took the ring home
and gave it to his wife for safekeeping
after telling her it belonged to the chief

soon after that
the chief ordered sarkin barayi
the head of the thieves' union
to steal the ring from the home of no-lord-but-God

the head thief searched everywhere but found no ring
so he returned and told the chief
that the ring was cleverly concealed

the chief ordered every man to come out and repair
the city wall
and while they worked he sent an old woman
with a hundred thousand cowries
a hundred rolls of cloth
and a hundred head-dresses
for no-lord-but-God's wife
in exchange for the ring

the wife was enticed into giving up the ring
and the old woman hobbled back to the palace
her mission accomplished

the chief was thrilled to see his ring
and gave orders for it to be thrown into the river
where it was instantly swallowed by a gigantic fish

by sheer coincidence
the son of no-lord-but-God went a-fishing
in this river
and caught the very same fish
that had guzzled the chief's ring

back in his home
the boy cut the fish up and found a ring
embedded in its soft white belly
and he called his father to come and look

no-lord-but-God came, saw and marveled
at this unexpected sight –
that ring

205

again!
he exclaimed in a voice filled with awe
"indeed, there is no lord but God!"

almost immediately
the chief's courier arrived with a summons
for no-lord-but-God

unruffled
he made his way to the palace
and there he was admitted into the chief's reception room
where
instead of greeting the chief as the others had done
he said as always:
"there is no lord but God"

the chief enjoined silence on everyone
then ordered no-lord-but-God to return his ring
at once

the palace guards surrounded no-lord-but-God
so that if he failed to produce the ring
he would be killed

as cool and collected as you please
no-lord-but-God reached into his pocket
and pulled out the ring
which he presented to the wide-eyed chief

he scrutinized the ring
saw it was really his

and declared in reverential tones:
"truly, there is no lord but God"

then he divided the town into two halves
and gave one to no-lord-but-God to rule

* *Editor's note:* Variations of this tale occur in both Arabian and Persian traditions.

juyin-gatan-fara

a rich man had thirty slaves
and a son called juyin-gatan-fara

one day father and son were out in town
when a caravan came by

the boy sought to know who was riding in it
and was told it carried traders
so he asked the traders where they were headed
whereupon they answered:
"ashanti"

the boy declared he would go with them
and hurling away his hoe
gathered up his gown
and ran after the caravan like a dog after a cart

his father stopped him for a moment
to give him a mare
which he could sell for food along the way
then boy and mare trotted after the travelling traders

when they arrived in the first town
juyin-gatan-fara saw a man with a wound in his foot
and asked him what had caused it
whereupon the man said
a sickle had slipped and hurt him
while he was cutting some grass

so juyin-gatan-fara gave him the mare
in exchange for the sickle

in the next town
juyin-gatan-fara saw a man with a dog
and exchanged his new sickle for the man's dog

at the third stop juyin-gatan-fara found rooms in town
rather than camp out with the caravan traders

and leaving his dog at his lodgings he took a stroll
but there was a gwari woman in the house
and you know gwaris eat dogs

well she killed his dog and roasted it
and juyin-gatan-fara returned to find only the head left
but he said nothing to anyone

the next morning when he told the master of the house
he was ready to leave
he was wished godspeed
but he replied that someone had devoured his dog
so how could he have a safe journey?

the master expressed disbelief until he was shown the dog's head
and then he asked the gwari woman:
"guilty or not guilty of eating his dog?"

the woman owned up
and the master threw up his hands in despair
so juyin-gatan-fara asked to be given the woman
as compensation for his dog
and the master gladly granted his request

taking the gwari slave woman with him
juyin-gatan-fara rejoined the caravan
and just before they reached the next town
they saw a member of the _gardawa_* league digging beside the road

juyin-gatan-fara confronted him
but the _ba-gardi_* replied that he was seeking a snake
so juyin-gatan-fara offered to take the snake
in exchange for his slave
and the ba-gardi gladly agreed

next juyin-gatan-fara opened his leather bag
and placed its mouth over the snake's hole
while the ba-gardi beat the bushes on the other side
the snake slid out and spiralled into the bag
which juyin-gatan-fara tied up tight

before sallying forth with his new find

when he rejoined the other traders he gave the bag
to the caravan captain to hold for him
with an injunction that he let no one touch it

the captain consented
but when juyin-gatan-fara's back was turned
he told the other traders he was entitled to a peek
in return for keeping the bag safe
so saying
he untied the pouch
and the snake darted out and slipped into the bushes

when juyin-gatan-fara asked the captain for his bag
he saw at once it was empty
and said the captain had to pay for opening the pouch
and anyway he'd owned a mare when he joined the caravan

the captain agreed to pay
and handed over two of his horses at once

the next day
the caravan arrived in ashanti
and all the traders began to buy and sell goods
but juyin-gatan-fara held on to his horses
and when the traders were done
he still had the horses

on their return home
the caravan stopped in another town
and juyin-gatan-fara set out on a stroll

he came upon an old woman who was preparing strong potions
and he asked her for some water
but she said he could get it himself
when he insisted that she fetch him some water
she left after warning him not to look in her pot

the moment she'd left

he wondered what was so special about that pot
so he opened it to see what it contained
and immediately went blind

the old woman returned to give him the water
and then saw he had gone blind
so she put it to him

he'd been looking in her pot

he admitted that indeed he had been prying
like many travelers are wont to do
and he asked her to restore his sight
she wanted to know what her reward would be
so he offered her one of his horses
in exchange for a cure

she concocted a potion that made him see again
and he offered to buy her pot with his second horse
so she gave it to him
and taught him how to restore sight

he grabbed pot and potion and dashed after the caravan
when the other traders saw him carrying a pot
they wondered what had become of his horses

when the caravan stopped for the night
juyin-gatan-fara gave his pot to the captain
with an order not to open it

as soon as his back was turned
the captain turned to the others and said
he didn't see why the pot should not be opened
so he peered into the pot
and immediately went blind

he called out at once to one of his helpers
"ubandawaki
open that pot and peer inside"

ubandawaki did
and he also went blind

then the captain called out to another helper
"jagaba
open that pot and peer inside"

jagaba did
and he also went blind

ditto for all the other traders

juyin-gatan-fara returned to find
the caravan captain and all his helpers were blind
he told them it served them right
for disregarding the injunction he had given in the prophet's name

the next day as they were preparing to set out juyin-gatan-fara
approached the captain and said

"i've been to ashanti and back
unharmed
and though i brought back no wares
i did bring back good health"

he said the same thing to ubandawaki
jagaba
and all the traders who'd lost their sight

as the caravan drew closer to his home
only a day's journey away
the captain begged the boy to cure his blindness

juyin-gatan-fara asked him what he was offering
and the captain offered some of his goods
when the boy asked him how many pack asses he owned
the captain said a hundred
and the boy demanded forty in return for a potion

the captain eagerly consented

so the boy gave him the potion and his sight was restored

next ubandawaki begged the boy for a potion as well
and was asked how many pack asses he owned
he said he had eighty
and the boy demanded thirty in return for a potion

ubandawaki speedily assented
and he regained his sight

then came jagaba's turn
and soon all the traders followed suit
each paid for a potion with one or more pack asses
and each in turn regained his sight

so juyin-gatan-fara now proudly owned
pack asses and goods galore
and as he hurried to his father's home
the people saw him and marveled
at the boy who had set out with a mare
and returned heavily laden with pack asses and goods

the moral of this amazing tale is this –
you can profit from anything
if you know how to turn the tables around

---

* _gardawa_ - inhabitant of gardi
* _ba-gardi_ - wise man of gardi
* _juyin gatan fara_ is Hausa for "selling at a huge loss in the hope of making an even larger profit on the sale of the goods bought with the purchase money

the girl, the orphan and the djinn*

there once was a girl
the finest in town
a learned man advised her father

to let no-one but an orphan marry her

time ticked by
and the cute little lassie became a nubile maiden
whose hand in marriage
every young man in town sought in turn
but her parents heeded the wise man's words
and offered her to an orphaned boy who lived nearby

the other girls in town were jealous of
the most beautiful one
so they schemed wickedly
and one day they invited her to join them in gathering tiger-nuts
in the fields

each girl collected some tiger-nuts
and pretended to eat them
thus tricking the beauty into really eating hers

she did
and the others made tracks for home
taking the nuts back to their parents
thus the beauty was shamed into staying behind
to gather more tiger-nuts for her own parents
and while she was alone in the fields
a djinn came along and abducted her

when they returned home the other girls denied
ever having seen the beautiful one
so her parents believing she was dead
buried a mortar in their backyard

when the orphaned boy came to see them
he was shown the grave
and told that his fiancee was dead

on hearing this heart-breaking news
the orphan set out for his home
but met an old woman along the way
who halted him and reported that

his girl had been kidnapped by a *djinn*
and her so-called grave held a mere mortar

that night
the orphan went and dug up the grave
only to find a mortar inside
he knew then the old woman had told the truth
and he covered up the fake grave

in the morning he saddled his steed
and told his slave to load his camel with all the essentials
for a long and perilous journey

when that was done
the orphan mounted his steed
his slave led the camel
and they both set out in search of the beautiful girl

the good Lord put them on the right track
and soon they arrived in a town
where the orphan announced:
"oh wise people
look at me, my slave, my horse and my camel and tell me
who is the handsomest of us all?"

the residents replied:
"truly
none is as handsome as the girl
who passed by here two days ago
now that has to be
the most beautiful person in these here parts
and you will find her in the next town
but we doubt you'll leave there alive"

the orphan climbed down from his handsome horse
and carried his weapons to the blacksmith
who gave them all a keen edge

the following day

he went on foot and all alone
until he came to the place he'd been warned about

a secluded house stood there
he entered and found his girl inside
she asked him why he'd come
and he replied that he was following her

she told him he couldn't save her
and then she fed him before
concealing him in one of the *djinn*'s corn stores

soon after that
the *djinn* came back
and declared he could smell a man

the girl maintained he was mistaken
because she was the only human around

when night came
the *djinn* and the girl went to bed as usual
then the orphan crept out of the corn store
and stole into the house
feeling his way carefully to where the *djinn* was lying
beside the girl

a raging jealousy rose in his throat
and he struck at the *djinn* with his spear
but it buckled
and so did the knives
and all his other weapons
while the *djinn* slept on regardless

the orphan crawled back to the corn store
where he concealed himself again

in the morning
when the *djinn* left home to hunt
the orphan returned to town
and had his weapons repaired

215

at night
he tried again to stab the *djinn*
again and again and again
but all to no avail

the next morning
the *djinn* left home as usual
and the orphan asked the girl to reveal
where the *djinn*'s life was concealed
but she didn't know and promised to find out

the orphan crept back into the corn store
just before the *djinn* returned
and that night in bed
the girl said to the *djinn*:

"oh husband of mine
can i ask you something?"

he told her to ask away
and she did -

"oh husband of mine
all i would like to know is:
where do you hide your life?"

the *djinn* replied with an ugly grin:
"oh that
is a long way away"

sweetly and seductively
the girl smiled and said:

"oh husband of mine
i know that already
but i must know the precise spot
or i fear i'll die"

and she looked into his bloodshot eyes
so he answered as softly as he could:

"oh wife dearest
pray, do not die
i will tell you my secret -
my life is hidden in a white gazelle's horns
and when other animals have had their turn at the water-hole
and it is really peaceful and dark
the white gazelle goes to drink at such-and-such a lake
oh wife dearest
that's all there is to tell"

the orphan overheard all this
from the corn store where he was hiding
and the following day
he sneaked off to town
to borrow a bow and arrow
then he went down to the lake and waited

before evening
the animals came down to drink
then withdrew
and at dusk
a graceful white gazelle stepped out

the orphan took aim with his bow and arrow
and the gazelle dropped to the ground
he used his knife to finish it off
then sliced off both horns
and carried them to the *djinn*'s house

there
he discovered the *djinn* was dead
so he took back his girl
lifting her up on to his camel
with the slave to lead her on
while he mounted his steed
and returned home
to present her proudly to her parents

the learned man addressed the girl's father thus:
"had you disregarded my advice

and married her off
to a man whose parents still lived
instead of to an orphan
as i advised
that man would never have risked his own life
to save her
he would have had his own parents to consider."

---

* *djinn* - genie, in Arabian tales, a spirit/goblin with strange powers

the ugly wife

there was once a man who had a plain wife
the ugliest woman in the whole town
this couple lived in such abject poverty
he didn't own one proper gown
and she owned no decent clothes at all
in fact they never knew where their next meal was coming from

one day he built a hut away from their house
and told her to close up the entrance
after he went in
to live like a recluse for forty days and nights

the wife sealed up the entrance with clay
and he prayed and fasted the whole time he was there
on his last night in seclusion
he had a strange dream which said
if he prayed for three things
they would all come true

at dawn the next day
he called to his wife to let him out
so she hewed down the clay door and freed him

he told her all about the dream he'd had
and she pondered this
and then said he should pray for her to become beautiful

that night he prayed as he was bidden
and in the morning
his wife had ceased to be ugly
and was now a breathtaking beauty
the like of whom could not be found in the land

news of this striking transformation spread
like bush fires in the *harmattan**
the chief heard it and sent someone
to bring her to the palace

the poor husband was overwhelmed by hopelessness
when the chief usurped his wife
until he recalled he still had two prayers left

so he prayed for his wife to be made a monkey
just as the chief was preening himself in preparation
for possessing his new bride

the chief went into the woman's room
expecting to see a ravishing beauty on the bed
but beheld a monkey instead
he was so furious that he foamed at the mouth
as he made his slaves remove the monkey
and take it to the poor man's house

when he saw his monkey-wife
he wished that things had remained the same
so he prayed for her to go back to the way
she used to be
before the dream
and his prayer was answered when the monkey became
his frightfully ugly wife

now he prayed for food and he prayed for clothes
and other things besides

but these went unanswered because
he'd already made the three requests
he had been promised in the dream

full of regrets he told himself
that he had learned a valuable lesson
any man who took a woman's advice
would surely get into trouble

---

* *harmattan* - a season in West Africa that is characterized by windy,
dusty and arid weather. Wild fires are not uncommon at this time as
most of the vegetation is dry and highly combustible.

auta and the ogre

once there was a couple who had two children:
an older girl
and a younger boy called auta

in time
the parents passed on
leaving the boy in his sister's care

the children left home
and many adventures later
they arrived in a new town
and stayed in an old woman's home

she told them to leave while they could
as the town was not a pleasant place to be in
but auta insisted that they would stay

the old woman's hovel lay on the way to the well
and in front of her home was an entrance hall
in which auta said that he would sleep

she said it was unthinkable because

the ogre in the town demanded a daughter of the chief
as yearly tribute
before allowing the residents to draw water from the well

auta insisted he would sleep in that hall
so he took a bag of stones from the old woman's house
then lit a fire in the entrance hall
and heated up the stones

at night
the ogre emerged to seize the chief's daughter
who had been put out for him

he set her down beside the well
then returned to stalk the streets of town
challenging anyone who dared to take him on

auta heard the ogre drawing near
and he accepted the challenge
loud and clear

the astounded ogre drew nearer still
so that the old woman hid herself among her calabashes
just before the ogre came up to her gate
and bellowed his challenge in clumsy language
once more

now the poor woman fainted dead away
but bold as brass auta bellowed back
he would take on the ogre
and beat him besides

this made the ogre mad as a hornet
and he began to break down the door of the hall
but auta said to step back a bit
so they could play an engaging game
before the ogre ate him for dinner

as soon as the ogre stepped back
auta took a stone from the fire and threw it at him

he caught it in his mouth and swallowed it whole
so auta threw another stone
and another
and another
until the ogre was so groggy from swallowing those heated stones
that he collapsed in a careless heap
just as auta threw the last stone

now he went over and cut off the ogre's head and tail
and then he went to the well
from where he took the chief's daughter to the old woman's home

next he sent his sister to get water from the well
and they sprinkled it over the old woman
thus reviving her

early the next morning
the women of the town went down to the well to get water
and on the way there saw the ogre lying in the street
so they dropped their pots
and hotfooted it back to town

soon the news was carried to the chief
by his courtiers who cried:
"the ogre rejected the girl he was given!"

the chief rallied his warriors round ·
with the aid of a talking drum
and twenty horsemen went to attack the ogre
but saw his fearful figure
and dashed away

a single warrior approached the chief
and asked to be given the kolanuts of battle
for he was ready to slay the ogre or die

he received the kolanuts of battle
and mounted his horse
dug in his spurs
welcomed death

and rushed off to destroy the ogre

on reaching the spot where the ogre's body lay
he saw it was without a head
so he turned back and told the chief
that the ogre had already been killed

the townspeople ran down to see for themselves
and there beside the ogre's head
they found auta's forgotten shoes

the chief ordered a drum to be beaten again
and when all had been summoned
he made them try on the shoes in turn

they fitted no-one and so the chief asked
if any strangers were in town
a man in the crowd recalled
he'd seen a girl and a boy the previous day

so the chief sent some men to find those two
and they returned with auta and his sister
when auta tried on the shoes
they fit him perfectly

when the chief asked him for the ogre's head and tail
he went to the old woman's home to fetch them
and also brought back the chief's daughter

the chief was delighted to see his daughter again
and he gave her to auta as his wife
in exchange for auta's sister

the town he divided into two
keeping one part for himself and giving the other to auta
as well as the title of galadiman gari
and then he married auta's sister
while auta married the chief's daughter

big andu and little andi

a man once had two wives who gave birth to two boys
on the same day: one in the morning the other in the afternoon

come naming time
the one who was born in the morning was called andu-babba
and the one who was born in the afternoon was called andi-karami

the two boys looked as alike as two peas in a pod
and when they became older their father built two huts for them
he planted a durumi tree at the door of andu-babba's hut and a
chedlya tree at the door of andi-karami's hut

andi-karami's mother passed away
so his father put him in the care of andu-babba's mother
and from that moment
the boys were inseparable
and always shared their food

when they grew older still
their father found wives for them
and they had a double wedding

immediately after the ceremonies
andi-karami went over to andu-babba's house
and they talked till daylight was fading
then andu-babba said it was high time he saw his brother off

andi-karami said he was surprised at his brother
for interrupting their friendly chat
so andu-babba said he didn't want to keep andi-karami
from his new bride

now the two of them went to andi-karami's house
where they talked the night away
and in the morning they still were not done

andi-karami made his wife get him water for a wash

and then he went with his brother to the latter's house
there andu-babba warned him against women
calling them surly unreasonable creatures
and he advised andi-karami
to spend more time with his wife

andi-karami accepted this advice
and always spent the night at home
although he still visited his brother morn and eve
and they still ate their meals together

but andu-babba's wife didn't like to see andi-karami
sharing her husband's food
so one day after she had finished cooking
she set the food before him like a dutiful wife
but just before he could tuck into it
his brother appeared

andu-babba invited his brother to share his food
but andi-karami was saddened to see
his brother had been about to eat without him
and so he claimed that he was too sick to eat

then he returned home and got a slave to saddle his horse
and he rode over to andu-babba's house to say goodbye

when his brother asked him where he was headed
andi-karami said he didn't know
but this much he knew:
whenever his chedya tree lost its leaves
his brother would know he no longer lived

andu-babba couldn't believe his ears
but his brother jumped on his horse and rode away

a little later
andi-karami and his slave came to a wild plum tree
with two plums on it
now he ordered his slave to pluck one plum
and leave the other for andu-babba

the slave picked one plum off the tree
andi-karami ate one half and gave the other to the slave

later they came to a shea-nut tree with two nuts on it
andi-karami ordered his slave to pluck one nut
and leave the other for andu-babba

next they came to a town where they stopped for the night
and at the house where they stayed
the people killed four chickens for dinner
but when andi-karami was offered the chickens
he gave two back with a request that
they be reserved for him on his return

in the second town
a ram was slaughtered for them
but andi-karami gave half of it back
to be kept until he returned

in yet another town
an ogre lived
who had to be appeased annually with a food gift:
a daughter of the chief
no less

andi-karami stayed with an old woman in this town
when he asked for a bucket with which to draw water for his horse
she told him to discard the idea because
an ogre lived inside the well

andi-karami maintained he must have a bucket
so the old woman gave him one
and he went down to the well
where he found one of the chief's daughters waiting to be eaten
by the ogre

he lowered the bucket into the well
and at the bottom
someone caught it
but andi-karami called out:

"whoever you are
come on out here
and we'll fight"

the ogre then replied:
"pull up the bucket but
you'd better leave because i'm coming out"

andi-karami put down the bucket
drew his sword and waited

when the ogre stuck his head out of the well
andi-karami sliced his head straight off
and immediately
the well overflowed
and flooded the entire town

andi-karami cut off the dead ogre's tail
then sent the chief's daughter home
and made his slave take water to the old woman
while he himself returned with the ogre's head and tail

in the morning
the people found their town flooded
and the chief's daughter recounted
how she'd been rescued
when asked where the stranger had gone
she said he was at the old woman's house

the chief sent some men to fetch him
and the astonished andi-karami went to the palace
where wedding preparations had begun

the chief thanked andi-karami over and over
and in gratitude gave him the title of yarima
and let him marry the daughter
he had rescued from the ogre
then the chief gave the young couple a house to live in

not long after that

a flock of guinea-fowl came from the hill behind
when the chief learned of this
he ordered everyone to drive the birds away

andi-karami mounted his horse
and with the others he galloped after the guinea-fowl
when the birds reached the hill
it opened wide
and they flew through the hole which suddenly appeared
andi-karami also went through
and the opening closed behind him

the other horsemen rode back to town without him
and told the people the yarima was dead

at that precise moment
a leaf fell from andi-karami's chediya tree outside his hut
andu-babba was passing by when he noticed this
and immediately realized his brother was dead
so he called for his slave to saddle his horse

andu-babba came to the wild plum tree with a single dried plum
and he told his slave to pick it because
his brother had left it for him

they came also the shea-nut tree with just one nut
and again he told his slave to pluck it because
his brother had left it for him

they came to the first town
and stopped at the same house where andi-karami had stayed
the occupants of the house greeted him warmly
and told him to take the two chickens he'd left the other time

the same thing happened with the half of a ram
when he arrived in the second town

then andu-babba came to the town where the ogre had been killed
and the people hailed him as the yarima returned
from the cave in the hill

news reached the chief
and he demanded some drumming and horn-blowing
to mark the return of the yarima

on the next day
the guinea-fowl reappeared
again the chief learned of this
and ordered everyone to drive the birds away

now andu-babba followed the yarima's drummers
and horn-blowers in the chase
but after all the other horsemen had turned back
andu-babba galloped on after the guinea-fowl
until the birds got to the hill
and flew through the opening which suddenly appeared
and closed behind them

andu-babba struck the hill with his sword
it opened again and his brother strode out
and said he was andi the slayer of the ogre
andu-babba said he was the slayer of the hill
then the two clasped each other's hand
and returned to the town

as they arrived
people were saying the yarima had a double
when they entered the palace
the chief said the two men had to be brothers

so andi-karami presented his elder brother to him
and the chief bestowed the title
of galadiman-gari on andu-babba

andu-babba and andi-karami never went back
to their home town but stayed in their new home
as galadiman-gari and yarima

death and the merchant

there was a clever merchant
who was also the wealthiest man in town
he owned a huge house
and plenty of property
cattle camels sheep and goats
slaves and other wares

one day he went to consult a soothesyer
and was told
he would be rich and successful for many years
but his life would end on a friday
in a particular month of a particular year

since this date was still a long way off
the merchant did not fret
but slowly the prophecy penetrated his thoughts
and as the day drew nearer
he became real scared

when the ominous month came
he refused to leave his house
but every market day
sent his most trusted slave to buy and sell for him
and to carry out his commands

market day was always on a friday
and nothing strange happened on the first two market days
the slave did his master's business
and reported duly back to him
but on the third market day
as the slave moved among the crowd in the market place
whom should he bump into but death himself
the slave was so disturbed
he couldn't reply to death's greeting

he rushed home to tell his master what he had seen
and the merchant was at first incredulous
but then he started to fear

death had indeed been seeking him
so he asked the slave if death had spoken to him

the slave admitted he'd been too scared to return death's greeting
and the merchant asked him if death had been looking for someone
but the slave said he didn't know
because death had seemed to appear from nowhere

the merchant pondered this in his mind
and decided that death had been seeking him
so he thought if he stayed away for one more market day
he would disprove the soothsayer's prophecy

the merchant owned a house in a distant hamlet called
tudun malga
so the next day he summoned his trusty slave
and confided in him saying
he would disguise himself
go to tudun malga and stay there
until the month was over
and he swore the slave to secrecy
even his wives were to be kept in the dark
about his hide-out

the slave vowed he would tell no one
then the merchant added to the deception
by ordering the slave to wear his master's clothes
and walk the streets
to make people think the merchant was still in town

the next day
the merchant dressed like a poor man
and stole away to tudun malga

the slave who looked like the merchant
wore his clothes and went about the town
fooling the people completely for five whole days

when the fateful friday came round
the slave was strolling in the merchant's clothes

when all of a sudden
the figure of death appeared before him
and greeted him once more

recalling the prophecy about his master
the slave feared that death had mistaken him for the merchant
and would now take his life
but in the end he found his tongue and said
he was ready to go with death

but death denied having come for him
so he said if it was the merchant that death was seeking
he had gone somewhere beyond death's reach

now death said slowly:
"no, my son
it isn't your master i am seeking
but someone else
i do have an appointment with your master
in the evening
not right now
and anyway we aren't meant to meet here
but in tudun malga
as was decreed from the very beginning"

the boy and the angel azrael

a mallam* had a boy-servant
to whom he said one day:
"go to the chief of butchers
and get the money he owes me
and no loitering on the way
you hear!"

the boy set out at once
running along the road
he met an old man carrying a raffia bag
and ran past him with the impatience of youth

but he found that whenever he turned round
there was the old man just behind
so out of respect
he offered to carry the old man's bag

but the man refused
saying the bag contained the lives of men
and the boy would not be able to lift it up

as they walked on together
the old man asked the boy where he was hurrying to
and he replied that he was on his way to collect
money owed to the mallam*
by sarkin fawa the chief of the butchers

the old man said he was also on his way to the sarkin fawa's
to take his life
and he advised the boy to get his master's money that day
or it would be too late
but he warned the boy not to say a word to anyone
about meeting the old man

the boy skipped ahead and when he looked back
the old man had vanished
so he ran to the town
saw the sarkin fawa in the slaughter house
and gave him the message from the mallam*

the sarkin told him to sit down and wait
and then he could take some meat to his master
as part-payment of the debt
but the boy insisted he must have all the money at once

the sarkin went on working
and did not see the old man appear
no-one but the boy saw him

abruptly the sarkin fawa stopped and said
he was feeling sick and so would go home
 while the boy would follow to collect his master's money

they both left together with the old man following silently behind
on arrival at his house he gave the boy the money
then hurled himself on the bed

while the boy was counting the money
the old man entered the room
took a cudgel from his bag
and struck the sarkin on the temple
next he drew a knife with which he slit the sarkin's throat
then put something on the wound to hide it
and stop the blood from gushing out

only then did the boy recognize azrael the angel of death
and he asked the angel not to conceal himself
whenever he came to take the boy's life

the angel said that would be hard on the boy
and it would be better if the boy didn't see him
on the day he was due to die

but the boy persisted with his plea
and so the angel agreed to grant it

then the boy took the money to his master
but said nothing about meeting the old man

years passed without his ever seeing the angel azrael again
and his parents arranged a suitable marriage for him

on the wedding day he was sitting in the best man's house
when the angel suddenly appeared

the boy saw him and his heart sank
he turned to tell his friend he had to go home
the friend insisted he couldn't leave just then
because everything was ready
it was wedding time

the boy claimed there was something he had to do
and hurried home

with the old man in tow
the boy rushed into his room
sent for his parents
and asked them to forgive him for any wrong he had done

they did
and he asked his elder siblings to forgive him too
which they did
finally he sought forgiveness from his younger siblings
and got it

when everyone else had left
the angel of death came in
and holding a knife to the boy's throat
told him to prepare to die

the boy said he was indeed ready
and the angel repeated his grim warning
again the boy said he was ready
and still the angel repeated his grim warning
and the boy said he was ready ready ready

then the angel said to him
"now rise
ant say how long you would like to live"

he did
and the angel azrael said
"take more years"

he did
and the angel azrael said
"more still"

the boy added to the number
and the angel azrael said
"more."

when the boy replied that he was content
the angel said

"ok son
on the day i return
you will not see me or know i am there"

and ever since
azrael the angel of death is never seen by men

---

* *mallam* - Moslem scholar and divine

HAUSA FICTION

women-like-lies

once there was a man called kariya-mata-ke-so
who went looking for a wife
although the only clothes he owned was a loin cloth
and he had no money to his name

before he went wife-hunting
his friend told him it made no sense to seek a wife
if he had no money
it was like hunting gazelle without a hound

but kariya-mata-ke-so said he had a good plan
and off he went to a village where he was unknown
he got a gullible rich man to lend him so many things:
a pair of pants, a gown, a turban, a sword-sling and a horse
also a big pot of honey and ten calabashes of kola nuts
which he promised to return in two days' time

quickly he donned the borrowed clothes
and strode out in style with the rest of the borrowed stuff
riding into a village he stopped at a house and said
"peace be with you."

the people in the house replied
"and with you be peace –
welcome."

kariya-mata-ke-so now dismounted
and his horse was led away
they showed him a hut to stay in
but when he came out to look at his horse
he hollered at whoever had tethered it with a rope
a boy admitted it was he
and pleaded ignorance
so kariya-mata-ke-so gave him a tasselled sword-sling
from timbuctoo
saying that was used to tether horses back home

now that boy was the younger brother of the girl
                kariya-mata-ke-so wished to marry
and he scurried off to give his sister the good news:
the stranger who had come to marry her was rolling in money

when she asked him to explain
he told her the man had his horse tethered with a tasselled
                sword-sling instead of a rope

the girl's eyes gleamed with glee
as she followed her brother to kariya-mata-ke-so's hut

while they were there the stranger's horse whinnied
and he sent the boy to get its food from the hut

he returned to say he had found no horse feed
only some kola nuts and a pot of honey
but kariya-mata-ke-so's haughty reply was
"people feed horses kola nuts and honey back where i come from"

the boy gave the kola nuts and honey to the horse
who knew enough not to eat that

but the girl was too excited to think
and ran to her parents to report she had found a spouse

they wanted to know why she had chosen him
so she told them all about the tasselled sword-sling
and the kola nuts and honey for his horse

237

they were as thrilled as she
and told her to hurry up and marry the man
before he changed his mind

kariya-mata-ke-so married her and took her home
then went to return the rich man's things
the girl saw her new husband coming back in his loin cloth
and asked him what had become of all his finery

kariya-mata-ke-so hollered:
"you dummy
don't you know my name is women-like-lies?
a horse can't eat kola knuts or drink honey
and as for being tethered with a tasselled sword-sling
that's foolishness
woman
if i hadn't lied to you
i wouldn't have won you
would i?"

the girl's replied quick as a gunshot:
"of course not!"

her husband said smugly:
"girl
you got what you deserve
this loin cloth you see
that's all i own in this world
so there!"

the householder snd the three blind beggars

there was a blind man who lived by begging
and one day he got enough alms to last him the whole day
but rather than return home
he went to a mansion to beg for more money

the mansion owner said he had nothing for the beggar that day
so he asked to be shown out of the house

and as he groped his way down the steps
he fell
and cursed a purple streak
while the householder laughed

the blind man got up and went home
unaware that the mansion owner was following him

at his home the blind man met his two blind friends
and related to them the story of his mishap
while the mansion owner listened undetected

the three blind beggars went in and began to eat their dinner
but the intruder slipped his hand into the dish
startling them so that they screamed and searched the room
but he climbed up to the rafters and concealed himself

satisfied that they were alone
the beggars shut the door and brought out a big bag of money
the mansion owner then tried to steal some
but the blind men seized him and screamed for help

the neighbors came running
and right away the intruder closed his eyes
pretending to be blind
and screamed along with the other three
so that when the neighbors forced open the door
they saw four blind men clasping one another's hands

the neighbors asked them to explain their action
and instantly the mansion owner piped up
saying he had a complaint against his companions
but he would only bring it before the chief

so the neighbors took the four men to the chief
and there the mansion owner said:
"long live the chief
i beg you to give each of us a hundred lashes each
starting with me"

the chief ordered his men to mete out the punishment

but after only two lashes
the mansion owner opened his eyes
and said he had something to confess

the chief gave him the go-ahead
and the mansion owner said:

"four of us go a-begging every day
and we combine our alms always
recently we decided to divide what we got so far
but my three companions tried to cut me out
so we started fighting till the neighbors came

now we also break into houses and steal

you see we really aren't blind at all
we just close our eyes and pretend
if you give my three colleagues a hundred lashes each
you will find they will open their eyes just like me"

the chief gave orders for the flogging to begin
so his men set upon the three blind beggars
who yelped and leaped with pain
while the mansion owner kept telling them to open their eyes
and the whipping would stop
or else if they refused to tell the truth
they would find the pains of purgatory much worse
than the pains of this world

the chief's men went on beating the beggars
while the mansion owner taunted them cruelly
the blind beggars bellowed like wounded bulls
until they had all received a hundred strokes each

they were now painfully weak
and still blind
so the mansion owner advised the chief to chastise them further
because they were determined not to confess

so the chief called for the beggars' money to be brought before him
it was and he split it into four

giving one part to the mansion owner
and keeping three parts for himself
then the three blind beggars were chased out of town
to their great amazement and rage

one good turn

two friends always ate their meals
and went around together
like needle and thread
one was a chief's son
and the other a rich man's son

the rich man had two magic rams
and one day while his son was walking with his friend
they came upon the rams

the chief's son wanted to know who owned them
so his friend told him they belonged to his father
and couldn't be found anywhere else
the chief's son sought to know why they were so special
so his friend said his father could cause the death of anyone
who sold or ate the rams or acted as witness

then the rich man's son offered his friend one of the rams
but the chief's son declined
saying he didn't want to die
but his friend urged him to take the ram
claiming his father had arranged it

so the chief's son took a ram then slaughtered it
and shared it among his family

the other ram ran home bleating
and the rich man told all his sons
that one of them must have taken a ram
and he was going to concoct a deadly dose
for anyone who killed the ram or ate it
or simply watched

his son begged him not to prepare a potion
because the chief's son being his good friend
might send some of the ram to him
and the rich man's slaves who often went to the palace
might be served some of the ram as well
so the rich man's son claimed he and the slaves would be killed
for the sake of a single ram

his father agreed to give up his plan
and the son ran off to tell his friend
how they nearly died for the sake of a ram
the chief's son vowed to repay his friend's kindness some day

some time after that
the two friends went on a stroll again
and the chief's son suggested they went to pay their respects
to the ladies of the palace

they both went into the women's quarters
and saw many ladies gathered there
the rich man's son wanted to know whose wives they were
so the chief's son told him they belonged to his father

the rich man's son looked like a child let loose in a toy store
so his friend took him out and asked
which one of the women he wanted

the rich man's son said they would both go in again
then he'd stop at a door and say he was thirsty
and that would be his chosen girl's door

so they both re-visited the harem
and the rich man's son stopped
at the door of one of the chief's favorite wives
and said he was thirsty

the chief's son told the girl to give his friend some water
and as she went to get it
he followed her into the hut and there he told her
that his friend was interested in her

she said the feeling was mutual
but as the chief was sleeping with her that night
she would arrange a rendezvous with the chief's son
the following night

in the evening of the next day
the chief's son found a slave girl who was as tall as his friend
and gave her some good clothes
while the rich man's son wore a gown, pants and cap all in white
then swathed his head with a white cloth
and with the slave girl he set off for the palace

they both went in
and changed clothes
then the slave girl left in a man's gown and pants
while the rich man's son settled down for the night
in the bed of the chief's favorite wife
in the morning he left the palace safely
dressed in the slave girl's clothes and a veil

the trysts continued for a while
till the day the rich man's son visited the chief's wife
on the very night the chief meant to sleep there

the young man was sitting in the room
when the chief himself strode in

the astonished chief recognized the rich man's son
and twice he asked the young man why he was there
but got no reply

so the chief summoned his hefty guards
and ordered them to put the young man in chains
and then he added

"arrest my son too
this is his best friend
so he must be involved
tie him up as well
and in the morning i'11 kill them both
after all he is not my only son

i've a tribe of children
and i won't miss him"

an old woman overheard this
and hobbled down to the house of the chief's son
to warn him of his father's plan

the chief's son told his slaves to saddle his horse
and he asked for twenty cowries
then rode out to the old woman's house
and bought some peanuts from her

now he rode to the city gate
and called to the captain of the gate to open it
but he refused
so the chief's son unsheathed his sword and said
the captain should open the gate or be killed
he chose to live
and let the chief's son through

the young man rode into the woods
until he came to a ground squirrel's hole
then he dismounted and dropped peanuts into the hole
so that when the squirrel came out to eat the nuts
he caught it and took it back to town

there he saw people gathered around the palace
and he galloped straight through to where his father stood
the chief called for his arrest
but quick as a bullet
his son rode away
to the spot where his friend stood
in chains

then the chief's son called out:
"what about our bet?
you said you would get the chief's ring
i said i would catch a ground squirrel
and we both agreed that the one who failed
would have his head cut off at this gate

well i've got my squirrel
now where's your ring?"

and he pulled out the squirrel from his bag
this made the chief think the two friends had only been
playing games
so he gave orders for his son's friend to be freed

when the chains were removed
the chief sent for a fine horse from his stables
and handed over the reins to the rich man's son
then gave him a town to rule

the rich man's son thanked the chief profusely
and thereafter lived in this town
but whenever he felt like seeing his friend
he would ride into the chief's town in style

the merchant and the deaf- mute

a merchant weighed down with goods
was travelling when he met another man
who asked him if the goods were heavy

the merchant admitted they were
and the stranger offered to carry half of them for him

so the merchant put down his load
shared it into two
gave half to the stranger
and they both went off together till they came to town

the merchant then said he would take his things back
as he was nearly at his destination

right there and then
the stranger began to babble like a deaf- mute
the merchant tried to take back his goods
but the stranger held on to them

while they were struggling
some people tried to separate them and failed
so they were hauled off to court

there the *alkali** asked the merchant to state
his side of the story
and the merchant said:

"i was returning from a journey
and met this man along the way
he asked me if my load was too heavy
and when i replied that it was
he offered to carry half of it for me
so i let him help me
and we walked until we got to the town
then i said i would take back my things
as i had almost reached my home
but then he began to babble like a deaf-mute
and we started struggling
so these people brought us here"

the *alkali** asked the people what they thought and they said:
"clearly the merchant saw this poor man was a deaf- mute
and tried to take advantage of him"

the *alkali** asked the merchant if he had a witness
but he had none
so the *alkali** called him a liar
and sent him away

the merchant left and lodged in the town
where he began to trade again with the rest of his goods
a friend of his soon found him there
and asked what had become of most of his goods
for the friend had met him while he still had his wares

the merchant recounted his misfortune
and his friend asked him if the other man lived in town
and if he really could speak

the merchant answered yes on both counts
now his friend was as clever as they come
and he asked the merchant to go and tell the *alkali**
he had found someone who understood the language of deaf-mutes
the merchant and his friend went to see the *alkali**
who laughed heartily at what he heard
and then sent for the deaf-mute

he came to the court
and the *alkali** ordered the merchant to relate his tale
the merchant said he had already given his version
and now the deaf-mute should give his

so the usher jogged him and he started jabbering once more
and the merchant's friend listened for a while
then yelled at him to stop
and he did

then the merchant's friend said to the judge:
"alkali*
this man has been abusing you!"

the phony deaf mute then cried:
"it's a lie!"
thereby giving himself away

under the orders of the judge
he was arrested and flogged and forced to return
the merchant's goods

**alkali* - judge

the farmer and the gazelle

a farmer was returning home after a hard day's work
when he bumped into a friend of his
who asked how the work was going

the farmer said he would finish it the next day
but his friend told him he had forgotten to add: "God willing"

the farmer insisted he would finish his work the next day
whether God was willing or not

the following day
the farmer took his hoe and went to his farm
he finished one ridge and started another
when a gazelle suddenly sprinted in front of him

he flung the hoe at it in an attempt
to bring it down
but the gazelle escaped
with the hoe dangling from its neck

the farmer tried to retrieve his hoe
and pursued the gazelle all day long
but only in the evening did the hoe fall off
and he was able to get it back

on his way home
he ran into his friend again
who asked if the farmer had finished his work
he said he had not
so his friend asked him to explain

when the farmer told him about the gazelle and his hoe
his friend said he had it coming
because he had claimed he could complete his work
even if God wasn't willing

the farmer hung his head in shame
and vowed to say "God willing"
from then on

the chief and his slave's wife

a chief liked to climb on to the flat roof of his palace
to watch what was going on in the town

one day
he sighted a spectacular beauty in one of the houses around
he sought to find out whose wife she was
and learned she was married to one of his slaves

he sent for the slave and handed him a letter
with an order that he take it to a particular town
and return with a reply
the slave put the letter under his pillow
and early the next morning
he set out
forgetting to take the letter along

the chief had been waiting for his slave to leave
and now he left the palace
the slave's wife saw him and curtsied
then spread a rug on the floor for him to sit on

he told her straight off why he had come
he had fallen in love with her
the girl gasped in horror and asked
how her lord could descend to taste the spring
where his dog used to drink

the chief hung his head in shame
and hurrying home
he left his slippers behind

the slave had discovered he didn't have the letter
halfway to his destination
and when he went back to collect it
he saw the chief's slippers and realized why
he had been sent on this mission

in spite of his anxiety

he completed the errand
and when he came back
he was given a hundred *dinars** by the chief

he took this money to the market
and bought his wife some fancy clothes
then persuaded her to pack up her things
and visit her family

she was delighted
and her parents were pleased to see her again
but when a month passed and her husband hadn't sent for her
her relations knew he was angry with her

they went to the slave to find out why
he had repudiated his wife
but he declined to give a reason
and would not take her back

the girl's relations took him to court
and told the judge
they had given a fertile farm to the slave
but he had returned it without any increase

when the judge asked the slave for his own side of the story
he said he had returned the farm in better condition
than when he had received it
so the judge told him to go back to the farm

but the slave said he would not
because he had seen a lion's tracks in it
and he didn't want to be killed

the chief was present at the trial and he swore
the lion had never touched anything in the slave's farm
then he rose and got ready to leave

the slave agreed he would go back to his farm
because the lion had left it alone

the chief said as he was leaving the court
he had never seen a farm to rival the slave's
and neither the judge nor the girl's relations
realized the real meaning of that remark

---

dinar - basic monetary unit in Muslim territories

the chief'a son and his servants

a chief's son called maina
fascinated by reports of the famed beauty
of a neighboring chief's wife
set out to seek this woman called miriam

on the way he met a man who offered to serve him
maina wanted to know what his trade was
"stealing" replied the man
and maina accepted his offer of service

they walked along together
till they met another young man
who also wanted to serve maina

when asked him what he did for a living
the newcomer said he was a know-all
and maina accepted his offer of service

the trio travelled together
till they met another young man
who wished to serve maina as a listener
and he too was allowed to join the group

as they went along
they met one by one
a warrior

chichi layor

a ferryman
a carpenter
a catcher
and a thrower
maina accepted them all

they arrived at their destination
and lodged in an old woman's home
maina gave her some scent and a jar of attar of roses
and asked her to take them to miriam

the old woman took the gifts to miriam
and told her they came from a rich stranger
miriam put the presents away in her hut
and then she tied up a bundle of things:
a small piece of cloth
a reed screen
some kola nuts
some old thatch
some hay
the leaves of a kurna tree
and a bone

she told the old woman to take these gifts to maina
which she did
there the thief opened the bundle and called
the know-all to come and look at the things

the know-all saluted maina
then proceeded to explain the significance of miriam's gifts
the kola nuts meant that the neighboring chief's gate was guarded
by slaves
and whenever the chief wanted the gate opened
he would give the slaves kola nuts

the piece of cloth meant
that more slaves guarded the inner gate
and they didn't speak _hausa_* at all
so whenever the chief passed through
he would give them a roll of blue broad cloth

then the bone meant a fierce dog was there
and before the chief passed through
he always threw the dog a bone

the hay meant there was a horse
that whinnied when anyone appeared

the leaves meant one had to go under a kurna tree
to reach miriam's hut

the old thatch meant the sleeping-out shelter by her door
and her own door was the one with a reed screen

maina thanked the know-all for decoding miriam's message
and he planned to go to her that night

under cover of darkness
maina made his way to the palace
and at the gate
the guards demanded to know who he was

silently he handed them the kola nuts
and they prostrated before him saying:
"may the chief's life be long!"

maina passed through the outer gate
and at the inner one he was confronted by the slaves
so he gave them the roll of blue broad cloth
and they prostrated before him saying:
"may the chief's life be longl"

as he passed through
a big dog leapt up at him
so he threw it a bone
and it settled down to chew

later he came across the horse
and it gave a whinny
so he threw it some hay
which it began to eat

he passed below the kurna tree
and saw a sleeping-out shelter
not far from it was the doorway with a reed screen
he went through it and found miriam inside

while they were talking
they were overheard by the chief
and he demanded to know who was there with miriam

she said there couldn't be anyone with her
at that late hour
so the chief returned to his room

soon he heard their voices again
and when he called out to miriam
she said it was the mosquitos that were bothering her

the chief returned to his room once more
and again he swore he'd heard a man's voice
so he came out and called for his slaves
to catch the intruder in his wife's room
and the slaves started sprinting towards the chief

in the meantime
maina's servants were bickering in their lodgings
when the one who was a listener leapt up
and yelled for them to keep quiet
so that he could work

he listened and then declared
their master had been discovered in the palace

immediately
the thief sneaked into the palace
undetected
and made a beeline for miriam's hut

he told her to pack her things and get ready to leave
so she and maina gathered up her belongings
then the thief told them to hold onto his shoulders
as he led them out of the palace

undetected

they arrived at the old woman's home
and together with the others
they escaped from the town

back at the palace
the chief had ordered that the women's quarters should be
surrounded
and any stray living thing should be killed

the slaves went through the house with a fine-tooth comb
but found no-one
so the chief had someone make an announcement
to find out if any strangers were in town

someone said that the only place where any stranger stayed
was the old woman's home
so the chief sent for her
and she told him the strangers had left while she was sleeping

the chief gave orders for the mounting gun to be fired
and the horsemen assembled in front of the palace
the chief mounted his own horse
and they all set out to find the fugitives

maina and his men were at the bank of a big river
when they looked back to see a cloud of dust
and realized the game was up

but the thief called for the carpenter to prove himself
so the carpenter felled a tall tree
and began to build a canoe

but the chief's men appeared before he could finish his task
so the thief called for the warrior to prove himself
the warrior went forward with his spear, sword and shield
and fought their pursuers till the canoe was ready

when it was launched
the thief called for the ferryman to act

so he ferried everyone save the warrior across the river
then he returned to get the warrior
who had been holding off the pursuers
and ferried him across to the farther bank as well

the chief came to the near bank
and called across to the other side
"is miriam there?"

she replied that she was
so the chief ordered his men to get her

immediately
a hundred horsemen rushed into the river
and drowned
the chief gave another order
and two hundred more horsemen rushed into the river
and drowned

the *galadima** urged the chief not to give another order
or they would all be killed
so the chief asked if any of his men could change into an animal

one man came forward and became a hawk
then flew across the river
seized the girl and carried her off

the thief called at once for the thrower to prove himself
so he picked up a pebble
and hurled it at the hawk
hitting it in the head

the thief called for the catcher to come forth
so he caught the girl as she fell to the earth
and put her down on a mat

now
which was the smartest of maina's men?

---

* *Hausa* - a language spoken in West Africa
* *galadima* - commander of troops

bididi

once there was a man who married a pretty woman
the loveliest by far in the whole town
but he was so jumpy with jealousy
he lived in fear of losing her to another man

one day the young men gathered around to gossip
and all agreed that her beauty was unrivalled
one of the men then decided
he would get her to bestow her favors on him

he went home and counted out two thousand cowries
then took them to an old woman called tsofuwa
and asked her to give the money and his warmest greetings
to the beautiful woman
with this message:
he was in love with her

tsofuwa delivered both money and message
and told the beautiful wife of the jealous husband
that she would get much more
if she went to the young man herself

the beauty said that was fine with her
but could tsofuwa ask the young man what his name was?

tsofuwa took this reply back
and just as he was about to say his name
the wise old woman told him
not to be stupid as to use his real name
and she suggested an alias: bididi
which he agreed to use

the jealous husband had noted the frequent visits from tsofuwa
and he became apprehensive
so he moved his household out of the town
to the woods where he had built a house

one day they ran out of salt and locust bean

and as he was laid up with toothache
he sent his wife to town to stock up on food

she headed for tsofuwa's house
and asked her to fetch bididi

tsofuwa went to bididi's house
to give him the good news
whereupon he promised to pay her with kola nuts
and immediately counted out seven thousand cowries –
two thousand for tsofuwa
and five thousand for the beauty

then he followed the old woman home
and found the girl waiting there for him
they greeted each other most graciously
and tsofuwa told the man to take his date
to the husband's house in town
for it was empty and their privacy would be assured

the young man said that would be a dangerous thing to do because
the jealous husband was likely to come looking for his pretty wife

so it was better for her to go home

now he told the girl he would see her soon
and could she get her husband to build
a grass shelter far from her hut?

the girl completed her shopping in town
then returned to their home in the woods
and told her husband:

"maigida
you should build a grass shelter
in case a leper or wandering scholar stops over
who needs somewhere to sleep"

he agreed it was a good idea
so he built a grass shelter

and she complimented him on his clever handiwork

in the meantime
the young man told tsofuwa to find out
if the shelter had been built by the jealous husband

tsofuwa took some salt and locust bean to the beauty
and they talked out of the husband's earshot

the old woman returned to bididi with the good news
the grass shelter was ready and waiting
so the young man got together
a small gourd filled with guinea corn
a few heads of bullrush millet
an undressed skin slung over his shoulder
and a staff
and sallied forth

when he arrived at the beauty's house
he chanted at the door:
"God bless the inhabitants of this house
please spare a few scraps of dumpling or flour paste
for a poor man"

the jealous husband said to his wife:
"the poor scholar needs to eat
take him something
in the name of God"

so she took bididi some left-over food
and showed the grass shelter
he gobbled down the food and fell to the ground
groaning for all he was worth

the jealous husband came and tried to carry him up but couldn't
then asked him what his name was
"bididi" was his reply
the beauty told her husband to give him some ash-water to drink
but bididi ignored the drink
and lay on the floor listlessly

chichi layor

until they both left him alone

the beauty spent the day making a dumpling stew
and in the evening she asked her husband
if she could take some of it
to the poor scholar
he told her to go on and see
if she could get the poor thing to eat

so she went to the grass shelter and called out "bididi!"

the young man replied in a seductive voice
"so you have come my lovely"
and she whispered, "yes"

so he pulled her down to the ground and told her
to keep repeating:
"bididi get up and eat your stew"
then he began to make love to her
while she chanted impatiently,
"bididi get up and eat your stew
bididi get up and eat your stew
bididi get up and eat your stew"

but at the height of her lust
she forgot herself and started moaning
"oooh bididi you are killing me oooh -
oooh bididi i can't bear it!"

her husband's ears picked up the strange sounds
and he raced to the grass shelter –
where he fell upon bididi with a howl
but then decided to hide his humililation
as he pleaded in a pathetic voice:

"bididi
i beg you in the name of God and the Prophet
to tell no one about this
or i'll be made a laughing stock
please help me to carry our things

as we move back to town"

so the couple packed up their possessions
and moved from their house in the woods
to their house in town
and that was the end of the husband's jealousy

the two thieves and the chief

once there was a man
and his best friend was a thief who shared with him
all that he stole

when the thief teased his friend for reaping
where he did not sow
he said he would start stealing
on the very day the thief stopped
so the thief dared him to steal something
and he vowed he would do that in his own good time

one day as they were travelling together
they came to a town and found
people lamenting the death of the chief's mother

the thief's friend said this was the right time to steal
and would the thief prepare to retire from the trade?
but the thief looked incredulous

at the chief's house
all the courtiers were weeping
and the thief's friend asked
if in the whole town no man of learning could be found
to bring the chief's mother back to life

when the courtiers said there was no such man
the thief's friend offered to do it himself
so the chief promised to pay him a hundred of everything
                                        he asked for
and they both shook hands on the deal

then the thief's friend called for some chains
which he took to the chief's mother's grave
and ordered for a hole to be dug beside it

it was done
and he tied one end of the chain around his hips
and gave the other end to his helpers to hold
with the instruction that he should be pulled out
when they could feel him tug the chain
and then he crawled into the hole

soon he started dancing inside the hole
stomping and vibrating like a man possessed
when the people heard the din down below
they scurried to the chief with a report

minutes later
the thief's friend tugged the chain
and he was pulled out of the hole
sweating like a stuck pig
and panting like a champion sprinter after a hot race

eagerly they asked if he had restored the chief's mother to life
the thief's friend replied that it had been
a spectacular but successful struggle
and then he disappeared down the hole

the courtiers scurried back to the chief with an exciting report:
his mother had been revived

but was yet to emerge

soon after that
the thief's friend tugged again on the chain
and was pulled up to the surface
sweaty as another stuck pig

he claimed that he'd been crossed
and had to see the chief privately
so his helpers followed him to the palace
and left him alone with the chief

then he reminded the chief of the deal they had made –
he would get a hundred of everything he desired
and now he told the chief:

"i have brought your mother back to life
but i had the most violent struggle with your father
who held on to your old lady
insisting he must come back with her--
sarki
our deal was for one life
not two"

the chief replied:
"that's true
so let's forget the whole affair
and let my mother stay with her old man
please keep this to yourself and i'll see
you receive your payment in full
just wait in the next town
and it will be brought to you there"

the thief's friend said persuasively:
"your mother left very recently
so you don't have to see her
but i do think you should go down and meet your father
for a minute or two"

the chief was quick to refuse
saying he didn't ever want to see his father again
the thief's friend said he had guessed as much
and had decided to check with the chief first

for this the chief was profoundly grateful

when the thief's friend left
the courtiers came to the chief to say
they were happy his mother would soon be revived
but he told them he had sent the thief's friend away
and there was nothing more to say

in due course

the two thieves received their reward
and the thief's friend said to the thief:
"whoever steals on a small scale
will be the object of suspicion
but these here goodies will last us all our lives"

as the saying goes
no matter how smart one is
there is always someone smarter

the mallam and the fortune-teller

a mallam enlisted the services of a fortune-teller
who poured some dust on the floor
then levelled it with his hand
and stared at it in contemplation

after a long while
he said he saw a bush cow send the man to his ancestors
the mallam asked if it was really true
and the fortune-teller said he could tell from past experience
that his client wished to argue
and he warned the mallam to be watchful
which he promised to do

the years passed
and the mallam rarely remembered the prophecy
one day he was sitting at home
when people started screaming:
"there's a bush cow in the fields!"

all the men in the village went after the bush cow
but the mallam recalled the fortune-teller's warning
and so stayed away from the fields
concealed inside a corn bin all day

the other men caught the bush cow and killed it
then as they were dismembering it
one man requested the head as his share

it was given to him and he took it home
and dropped it into his corn bin
meaning to flay it later

but this was the same corn bin in which the mallam
had concealed himself
so the bush cow's head fell on him
and one horn perforated his chest killing him

in the morning
the owner of the corn bin came to retrieve the bush cow's head
and found the mallam's cold body inside

the people were puzzled by this discovery
until the mallam s wife explained
how a fortune-teller had predicted
that a bush cow would cause his death
and the prediction had been proved true

the people nodded sagely and said:
"our destiny is ordained from the day we are born"

the merchant and the pot of oil

a merchant planned to travel
but first he put all his money in a pot
filled with oil
then took it to a friend
to keep until he returned
but he didn't tell the friend that the pot contained money

the merchant was away for ten long years
during which time his friend found the oil
and the money

he cleaned the money and kept it for himself
then replaced it with pebbles
and poured back the oil

when the merchant returned
his friend welcomed him warmly
saying he'd been given up for dead

the merchant said he owed his return to the mercy of God
and two days later he came to get his pot from his friend
the oil looked like it hadn't been disturbed
so he thanked his friend and took the pot home

then he went straight to the market
and bought lots of things
promising to pay for them the following day

when he got home
he poured out the oil
but found only pebbles inside the pot

he berated himself for being foolish
and he was afraid to tell anyone his story
for fear that he'd been considered crazy
so he just worried himself into a frenzy

one day another friend came calling
and found him immersed in hopeless misery
the friend asked him what there was to be so gloomy about
and he said he would only tell him in confidence

so they went into the woods
and he told this friend how he'd been tricked
by the other friend
and now he sought the second friend's advice

he asked the merchant some questions
in skilled sleuth style:
did the merchant entrust his money to the first friend?
and was that friend still in town?
and did he have a son?

the merchant answered yes
on every count
and then his friend asked the final and crucial question:

what was the merchant willing to pay
if his friend could recover the money?

the merchant pledged a third of the sum
and a deal was struck

first the friend asked to see the fickle man
so the merchant pointed him out without letting him know
he was under intense scrutiny

the second friend studied this man
like a scientist studies a specimen under the microscope
and then he went and fashioned a wax figure of the fickle friend

next he took it to the merchant and said:
"place this in your bedroom
and go catch a monkey
then tie him to the waxwork
till he's so used to it
he'll struggle against a separation"

the merchant carried out these instructions
and returned to tell his friend
that the monkey and the wax figure were like siamese twins

the friend told him to ask the faithless friend
if he would let his son go to help the merchant in the market
the friend consented
and sent his son muhammadu with the merchant

the merchant took the boy to his house
instead of the market
and in accordance with the second friend's instructions
he hid the boy in his house
then took the monkey to muhammadu's father
and told him that his son had become a monkey
unexpectedly

the monkey saw muhammadu's father
and immediately clung to him like a leech
thinking he was the wax figure

the merchant exclaimed:
"*wallahi** although muhammadu is now a monkey
he hasn't forgotten his father!"

a crowd gathered to watch the curious spectacle
of the monkey glued to the man like nettles to clothes
in spite of people's attempts to separate them

the merchant told the spectators
that the monkey was the man's son
and should be left alone
then the merchant went home

the news spread like grassfire
and many more came to see for themselves
this monkey with a human father
soon muhammadu's father was engulfed in despair
and that night he went to the merchant and asked
if his son had really become a monkey

the merchant rejoiced to see the tables turned
and he replied with a question:
"why can't muhammadu become a monkey
when money can change into pebbles?"

muhammadu's father replied:
"all right you win
now send that pot of yours back to me"

the pot was sent to him and he put the money back inside
then poured in the oil
and returned the pot to the merchant

he checked to see that his money was intact
and then he returned the boy to his father
and went to pay his friend as promised
but the friend turned down the money
because he didn't want to catch the contagion of foolishness
from the merchant

moral:
don't ever place money in another person's care
unless witnesses are present

---

wallahi - Hausa exclamation signifying surprise or contempt

dan-kano and dan-katsina

dan-kano and dan-katsina were two daring rogues
one came from kano
and the other from katsina

one day dan-kano stripped the bark off a baobab tree
dyed it in the dye-pit
and beat it to a glaze
then wrapped it in paper so it could pass for good broadoloth

at the same time
dan-katsina filled a goatskin with pebbles
put a couple of hundred cowries on top
and bound up the top of the bag
then set off for the market

on the way
he met the other rogue
who asked where he was headed
so he said he was going to the market
and he asked dan-kano what he had for sale

dan-kano answered:
"oh the bluest broadeloth you ever saw"

so dan-katsina said:
"what a welcome coincidence
i was on my way to buy some broadaloth
and i've got twenty thousand cowries in my bag"

right there and then the rogues reached an agreement
and swopped their wares before they got to the market
each man thought he had outsmarted the other
and so they parted on a happy note
but when they had taken a few steps
each man stopped to see what he had received

it was then that dan-kano saw the sack of stones
and dan-katsina saw the bundle of bark
immediately they retraced their steps with the speed of wild horses
and bumping into each other
decided they were equally matched in craftiness
and would surely go far if they joined forces

so they teamed up together and hit the road
and when they came to a town
they got water-bottles, begging bowls and canes
and slipped into the role of blind beggars

they walked along till they were deep in the woods
and came upon some traders in a camp
then the two rogues hid themselves in a nearby bush

when it was dark
they crept out of the bush
and entered the traders' camp
disguised as blind beggars

they were allowed to stay
and when the traders drifted off to sleep
the two rogues carried away all their wares
and hid them inside a dry well

at dawn on the next day
the traders discovered their loss
and the two rogues claimed their water-bottles had also been stolen

this made the traders mad
and they yelled:
"we've lost all our wares

and yet you puny beggars are only concerned with your
water-bottles
go on get outta here!"

so the two rogues picked their way out of the camp
and when the traders left in despair
the rogues opened their eyes and ran
to the well where they had hidden the wares

they argued over who would go down the well
to get the traders' wares
when finally their greed overcame their mutual distrust
dan-katsina went down the well

dan-kano lowered a rope
and dan-katsina tied the goods to it
after which dan-kano pulled them to the top
and piled them in a heap away from the well
each time he returned to the well with a big stone
and stacked all the stones near the well

some time later
dan-kano called out to his colleague:
"dan-katsina
when you have sent up all the stuff
and you are ready to come out
just tell me and i will pull you up gently
so you don't scrape your skin against the side of the well"

dan-katsina replied "okay"

they lugged away till the last bundle had been hauled up
but dan-katsina did not reveal this fact
and told his co-thief that the next load would be the last
and would be bulky as well

after he said this he climbed into the last bale
and hid inside it
then dan-kano hauled it up and stacked it with the rest unaware
that dan-katsina was inside the bundle

now dan-kano went to where he had piled up the stones
and started flinging them into the well
in the belief that dan-katsina was still down there

while dan-kano was throwing stones
his colleague crawled out of the bale
and began to move the goods to another hiding place

dan-kano returned to find the goods all gone
to his great amazement
but his craftiness did not fail him now
and he had a bright idea:
the thief had to be in the vicinity still
and would surely need a beast of burden to cart away all that stuff

so dan-kano slipped into some nearby scrub
and began to bray like a donkey
instantly dan-katsina rushed out
expecting to see a donkey
but he saw his fellow rogue

dan-kano cried:
"dan-katsina you scoundrel"
and dan-katsina replied:
"dan-kano it takes a rogue to know a rogue"

they both gathered the goods together
and took them to dan-kano's house
then dan-katsina said he had to visit his home
and when he returned in three months' time
they would divide up the booty

dan-kano said that was all right with him
but two months later he dug a grave in his yard
and covered it up with broken calabashes and potsherds

then just before dan-katsina's return
dan-kano withdrew into this grave
and his family piled earth over the potsherds and calabashes

soon dan-katsina arrived

and asked to see dan-kano
when his family said he had died four days before
dan-katsina demanded to see his grave

at the graveside he wailed loudly
then resigned himself to the will of God
and advised dan-kano's family to cover the grave with thorns
so as to keep hyenas from digging it up

the family promised to do that the following day
and they showed dan-katsina his lodging for the night

they tried to make him most comfortable
serving him stew and dumplings and milk gruel
but he refused to eat anything

claiming that he couldn't eat with his friend dead

at midnight when everyone was sleeping
he sneaked out of bed and went to dan-kano's grave

he got there and began to claw the earth on the grave
and growl like a hungry hyena seeking food
dan-kano heard the racket from inside the grave
and scared of being eaten alive
he screamed an s o s

dan-katsina chuckled and called for him to come out
and when he did
the two scoundrels shared the stolen goods
equally

the caravan captain and his faithful wife

a caravan captain had a close friend
they were always found together except
when the captain went on his trading trips

now the captain's wife was consistently chaste

273

even in the face of other men's lewd advances
and one day when the captain and his friend were arguing
about women
the captain said he could count on his wife's fidelity always

the friend said he would prove the captain wrong
and so they bet on it right there and then
the friend claimed he would seduce the captain's wife
or give up his horse and concubine

the captain said that if his friend made good his claim
he would hand over all the asses, pack ponies, mules and goods
from his trading expedition

soon he went on a trading trip
without saying a word to his wife about the bet

his friend counted out ten thousand cowries
and sent them to the captain's wife –
three days later
he counted out another ten thousand cowries
and it went on like that till he'd sent her
fifty thousand cowries

when she received all that money
the captain's wife sent for the captain's friend
and when he came
she thanked him for his lavish gift
then asked him what he wanted from her

he replied that he wanted only her
so she asket him what he meant
and asked again and again
before he blurted out his desire
to sleep with her

unfazed
she said it was perfectly easy to arrange
and promised to see him that night
if he could find a meeting place

the man could hardly believe his luck
and he told her to meet him in his servant's hut
she agreed to be there without fail
and left

when darkness came
she sent for one of her slave girls
and dressed her in her own clothes, shoes and perfume
then packed her off to the captain's friend
with strict orders not to speak till she came home

armed with a razor
the captain's friend was already waiting
and licking his lips in lust
he saw the slave girl enter the hut
and believing she was the captain's wife
took her into his bed

when it was all over
he used the razor to make a small cut in her thigh
before they put their clothes back on

the slave went back to her mistress with the wound
which she dressed so that it soon healed
and she congratulated the slave for a job well done

later
the captain came back with a full caravan
but for three days he did not unpack his wares
then on the third day his friend came calling
and laid claim to the captain's goods

the captain asked for proof that he'd won the bet
so he told the captain to call his wife

his heart pounding like a newly-caught bird
the captain sent for his wife
with hanging breath
and asked her if it was true
she had slept with his friend

she said she had not
and rebuked him
for even believing that she could

just when his friend asked to see her thigh
she bawled him out for his boldness
then went and fetched her slave girl
while the captain looked like an undertaker's new assistant
for he feared he would lose all his wares
to his friend

his wife returned with her slave girl
and ordered her to bare her thigh
so she showed them the scar from the razor-cut
and then the captain's wife
contemptuously addressed the friend:

"you can now see where you laid your load
and it wasn't on me"

then she asked her husband if there had been a bet
and he said yes
so she ordered his friend to pay up his stake

the captain told his friend to hand over the concubine
and hold onto his horse
so the friend brought the concubine to the captain
who then gave the slave girl to his wife

she admonished her husband with these words:

"madugu
you shouldn't have doubted my fidelity
they say men chase women
but don't forget
women have their own minds as well
and if the woman isn't willing
then the man can't sleep with her
you know"

swiftsure

a farmer once went to a tuareg for a loan of five hundred thousand
cowries
he got the loan and told the tuareg:
"come and collect your money next year
if we are spared"

the months went by fast and when payment of the debt was
almost due
the farmer started a new farm
on the road down which the tuareg would come

on the day the tuareg was due to arrive
the farmer made his wife cook mutton stew and dumplings
and milk gruel and pancakes

next he went and caught a ground squirrel
then brought it home and tied it up
and set out to his farm

on the way he caught another ground squirrel
and took this one to the farm

much later when the tuareg came with his camels
he saw the farmer working on his farm
the farmer greeted him eagerly
and claimed he wasn't expecting the tuareg to arrive on that day
but he was sure his wife could put a meal together
somehow

then the farmer went and freed the ground squirrel
saying:
"swiftsure, do run along home to the mistress and tell her
we have a special guest
and she should make dumplings and stew and milk gruel
and pancakes"

the tuareg watched as he freed the squirrel
and then he added as an afterthought:

"and swiftsure
remember to tell the mistress to tie you up again
okay?"

the squirrel scuttled off
and the farmer and the tuareg talked for a while
then the farmer stood up and said it was time to go
so they went to his home
where the tuareg and his slaves were shown their lodgings
and served with splendid food

later
the farmer went to see him in his room
and was asked:
"where is swiftsure?"

the farmer said the ground squirrel was around somewhere
and the tuareg offered to buy it
but the farmer refused to sell
claiming it had cost him so much
and anyway he needed it on the farm
to run errands every now and then

the tuareg was suitably impressed
and he asked how much the squirrel had cost
the farmer said it had been expensive -
a million cowries
no less

but the tuareg wasn't to be put off
and he agreed to pay the price
he reminded the farmer of the five hundred thousand he was owed
claiming that he could pay the balance of five hundred thousand
in cash
right there and then

the farmer feigned reluctance at first
but then he agreed to sell the ground squirrel
for a million cowries
so the tuareg gave him the money
and received the squirrel in return

then tied it to his saddle
and set off for home on his camel

when he was three days' away from his village
he freed the squirrel with these words:

"swiftsure
take a message for me
scoot along to my house and say
we are on our way home
and they should cook lots of food"

the squirrel scuttled off into the woods
as soon as it was untied

the tuareg got home and found
he hadn't been expected
and he angrily asked why the food wasn't ready
when he had sent a message ahead of him

his family sought to know whom he had sent
and when he replied that it was swiftsure
they told him they had seen no one

the tuareg flew into a fury and accused them of lying
and it took the neighbors' intervention to quiet him down

time passed
and one day the tuareg went to the woods with some of his slaves
to round up his camels
suddenly he spied a ground squirrel
and exclaimed:

"*wallahi* look at swiftsure
when i sent him on an errand
he must have run into the woods!"

one of the slaves said respectfully:
"that's a ground squirrel like any other
they live in the woods and always stay away from people"

the tuareg let loose a string of curses
and said he was going to get the man
who had swindled him

---

* *wallahi* - Hausa exclamation signifying surprise, disgust or
contempt

the blind woman and the mallam

once there was a chief who decreed
all those found guilty of fornication or adultery would be killed
and their families' goods confiscated

when a blind unmarried woman got pregnant
it was reported to the chief
who ordered that she be brought before the judge

the woman was appalled by the news
and she sought the services of a mallam
to get her off the hook

she told him she had put her family's property in jeopardy
and implored him to prevent confiscation of the family's effects
even if she herself were sentenced to death

the mallam asked her to name his reward
if somehow he managed to get her cleared of any crime
she pledged to pay a hundred thousand cowries
and the deal was made

then he proceeded to give her instructions –
when the judge asked her who got her pregnant
she was to answer as follows:
"your honor!
i cannot name the man because i am blind
but his voice was like your voice

and i think you are he"

the blind woman thanked the mallam for his help

in time she was summoned before the judge
and placed in that part of the court reserved for women
the judge sent the *mufti** to examine her there
and when the mufti asked her who had gotten her into trouble
she replied:

"your honor
i cannot name the man because i am blind
but his voice was like your voice
and i think you are he"

the mufti went to the judge to say
he couldn't make out
what the blind woman was trying to say
so the judge said he would question her himself
and he asked her who had made her pregnant
again she replied:

"your honor
i cannot name the man because i am blind
but his voice was like your voice
and i think you are he"

the judge told the court he couldn't understand
what the woman was saying
and so he had to consult the chief

the judge told the chief
that he couldn't unravel the woman's statement
and the chief bellowed like an angry bull:

"look here, *alkali**
i know her family is very rich

but that is no reason to ravel up the case
send her in and i'll examine her myself!"

the judge brought the blind woman to the chief
and he asked her who was responsible for her pregnancy
she answered as before:

"your highness
i cannot name the man because i am blind
but his voice was like your voice
and i think you are he"

the chief growled at her:
"woman!
do you know whom you are addressing?
i am the chief of this town!"

she said as calmly as you please:
"i cannot see
and so i can only speak of what i heard
his voice was like your voice
and i'm sure you are he"

the chief summoned the judge
then told him the woman was mad
and should be released

so she was discharged
and returned home
when the mallam heard the news
he arrived at her door

and called out a greeting:
"salaam aleikum"
and she answered:
"aleikum salaam"

the mallam said he'd heard of her release

and she confirmed it was true
when he told her to give thanks and praises to God
she replied that only the Lord was benevolent
finally the mallam demanded the hundred thousand cowries

she had pledged to pay him

now the woman seemed to go berserk
as she screeched at the spectators:
"first he got me into trouble
and now he has come to ask for money
imagine that!"

the mallam exclaimed in amazement:
"am i also to be treated thus?
then may God curse you
and deny you sight a trillion times
and more!"

---

* *alkali* - Muslim judge
* *mufti* - Muslim scholar